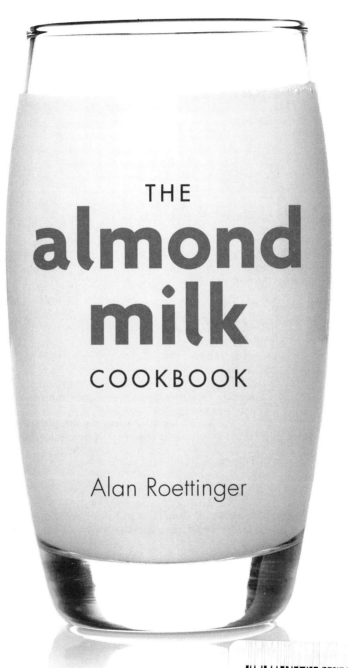

THE
almond
milk
COOKBOOK

Alan Roettinger

Book Publishing Company
SUMMERTOWN, TENNESSEE

Library of Congress Cataloging-in-Publication Data

Roettinger, Alan, 1952-
  The almond milk cookbook / Alan Roettinger.
    pages cm
  Includes index.
  ISBN 978-1-57067-326-9 (pbk.) — ISBN 978-1-57067-876-9 (e-book)
1. Cooking (Almonds) I. Title.
  TX814.2.A44R64 2015
  641.6'455—dc23

                                                              2015005578

Book Publishing Company is a member of Green Press Initiative. We chose to print this title on FSC-certified paper with 100 percent postconsumer recycled content, processed without chlorine, which saves the following natural resources:

  55 trees
  1,734 pounds of solid waste
  25,914 gallons of water
  4,778 pounds of greenhouse gases
  25 million BTU of energy

For more information on Green Press Initiative, visit greenpressinitiative.org.

Environmental impact estimates were made using the Environmental Defense Fund Paper Calculator. For more information, visit papercalculator.org.

Printed on recycled paper

Cover and interior design: John Wincek
Stock photography: 123 RF

Printed in Canada

Book Publishing Company
PO Box 99
Summertown, TN 38483
888-260-8458
bookpubco.com

ISBN: 978-1-57067-326-9

20 19 18 17 16 15   1 2 3 4 5 6 7 8 9

contents

Almond Milk in a Nutshell

A Brief History of Almond Milk

Almonds have been enjoyed by humans for thousands of years. The earliest varieties of almonds were found in China and were carried by traders down the ancient silk road to Greece, Turkey, and the Middle East. Their first appearance in North America came via Spanish missionaries who settled in California. Today, almonds are featured prominently in both sweet and savory dishes in cuisines around the globe, and there are more than thirty different varieties of almonds cultivated and enjoyed worldwide.

Almond milk, made from finely ground almonds and water, has been consumed from Europe to east Asia since at least as far back as the Middle Ages. In the days before the advent of refrigeration, cow's milk, which spoils very quickly, was a relatively rare and expensive commodity. Because it was so highly perishable, fresh cow's milk was always consumed soon after it was collected and used either as an addition to other foods or cooked and transformed into butter, yogurt, or cheese. Almonds, on the other hand, were easily kept and transported, and almond milk could be made as needed with little difficulty.

Many medieval recipes called for almond milk, and making the milk involved an uncomplicated process that the cooks of that period were well versed in. It entailed nothing more than combining one part ground almonds with two parts boiling water, allowing the mixture to steep, stirring it occasionally until cool, and then straining it to remove any large bits.

With the modern rise of vegetarianism and veganism, as well as the increased awareness of lactose intolerance and other health concerns related to the consumption of dairy products, many consumers have become keenly interested in nondairy milks. Soy milk became the rage during the 1970s following the publication of *Diet for a Small Planet* by Frances Moore Lappe. Since then, both the quality and accessibility of commercial soy milks have steadily gotten better. However, almond milk in particular has enjoyed a tremendous surge in popularity, especially since 2010, when greatly improved commercial almond milks became available. Sales of almond milk in North America have now overtaken those of even soy milk, due in part to soy sensitivities but mainly attributable to almond milk's superior flavor.

Health Benefits of Almonds

Almonds are among the most health-promoting foods known, providing biotin, calcium, copper, fiber, folate, iron, magnesium, manganese, omega-6 fatty acids, phosphorus, potassium, protein,

TABLE 1 Nutritional value of almonds per 100 g

PRINCIPAL NUTRIENT	NUTRIENT VALUE	PERCENTAGE OF RDA
Energy	575 Kcal	29%
Protein	21.22 g	16%
Total fat	49.42 g	165%
Cholesterol	0 mg	0%
Dietary fiber	12.20 g	30%

VITAMIN	NUTRIENT VALUE	PERCENTAGE OF RDA
Folate	50 µg	12.5%
Niacin	3.385 mg	21%
Pantothenic acid	0.47 mg	9%
Pyridoxine	0.143 mg	11%
Riboflavin	1.014 mg	78%
Thiamin	0.211 mg	16%
Vitamin A	1 IU	0%
Vitamin C	0 mg	0%
Vitamin E	26 mg	173%

MINERAL	NUTRIENT VALUE	PERCENTAGE OF RDA
Calcium	264 mg	26%
Copper	0.996 mg	110%
Iron	3.72 mg	46.5%
Magnesium	268 mg	67%
Manganese	2.285 mg	99%
Phosphorus	484 mg	69%
Potassium	705 mg	15%
Selenium	2.5 µg	4.5%
Sodium	1 mg	0%
Zinc	3.08 mg	28%

(Source: USDA National Nutrient Database)

selenium, vitamin E, and zinc. Although almonds are rich in fat, nearly all of it is heart-healthy monounsaturated oleic acid, the same type of fat found in extra-virgin olive oil that is credited with lowering LDL ("bad") cholesterol levels and helping to prevent cardiovascular disease.

Almonds also help to balance blood sugar. When consumed as part of a regular meal, almonds help lower the glycemic index of the entire meal and reduce the overall after-meal rise in blood sugar. This decreased blood sugar spike in turn helps protect against diabetes and cardiovascular damage. The skins of almonds are rich in potent flavonoid antioxidants, and when eaten in combination with the rich vitamin E present in the almond's flesh, the beneficial effects are multiplied.

The almond we know as a nut is actually a drupe, or stone fruit. It's binomial name is *Prunis dulcis.* Technically, almonds are the seed of a fruit, belonging to the same category of stone fruit that includes apricots, cherries, nectarines, olives, peaches, and plums. Be aware that people who are allergic to these fruits might have a similar sensitivity to almonds and vice versa.

The average serving of almonds according to the United States Food and Drug Administration (USDA) is 23 kernels. This is the equivalent of 1 ounce, ¼ cup, or about one handful (depending on the size of your hands) of almonds. The USDA Nutrient Data Laboratory states that 1 ounce of whole, shelled almond kernels contains 163 calories, about 14 g of fat, 6 g of protein, 6 g carbohydrates, and 3.5 g of fiber.

The Many Faces of Almond

The versatile almond is readily available in a wide array of forms. Although when making almond milk it's best to use whole, unroasted, natural almonds to obtain the highest nutritional value, almond milk can actually be made from almonds in any of the following commonly found forms:

WHOLE. Whole, shelled almonds are available natural (with the skins on) or blanched (with the skins removed). The skins are especially rich in flavonoids, a food component high in antioxidants that assists with scavenging free radicals. Flavonoids have been shown to help prevent coronary heart disease and provide anticancer activity. Blanched almonds, which are almonds that have been briefly doused with boiling water to loosen the skins so they can be easily removed, provide more aesthetic appeal in finished dishes. Both types of almonds are available raw or roasted and can be used as an ingredient in baked goods, cereals, confections, energy bars, grain dishes, salads, and main dishes.

SLICED AND FLAKED. Natural and blanched almonds are also sold sliced or flaked. They make delicious, nutritious toppings for cold and cooked cereals, cooked grains, and salads; wholesome additions to baked goods; and eye-appealing garnishes for both sweet and savory dishes.

SLIVERED AND HALVED. Available with or without skins, slivered and halved almonds add crunch to confections, cooked and cold cereals, salads, and stir-fries.

CHOPPED. Natural or blanched, chopped almonds are excellent for topping frozen desserts, savory casseroles, and sweet or savory pies. They also are terrific added to cooked grains, crusts, pie fillings, and stuffings. Use them as a crunchy coating instead of bread crumbs, or add them to cookies in lieu of other nuts or flavored chips.

MEAL AND FLOUR. Almond meal and flour can be made with either natural or blanched almonds. Use it as a thickener for gravies, puddings, and sauces or to partially replace some of the flour in baked goods. Almond flour is an excellent, gluten-free alternative to standard flour in baked goods and makes a good replacement for fine bread crumbs for coating foods.

BUTTER OR PASTE. With continued processing, finely ground almonds will eventually turn into almond butter, a delicious, versatile spread similar to peanut butter. Use almond butter in confections, cookies, dips, granola bars, pies, sauces, and savory dishes, or as a sandwich spread. A nearly instant almond milk can be made by blending almond butter with water. A good general ratio is 1 to 2 tablespoons of almond butter to 1 cup of water. Although not as tasty as freshly made milk from whole almonds, it works great in a pinch.

Riding the Almond Milk Wave

Some purists argue that almond milk is just a watered-down version of whole almonds with the fiber removed. Well, point taken. But a handful of almonds can't be poured on breakfast cereal, stirred into tea or coffee, or used in the myriad applications outlined in this book. Almond milk lightens, enhances, and enriches all kinds of food, making possible a broad array of creamy, healthy, nutritious, dairy-free, gluten-free delights. Why limit yourself when you can use both whole almonds *and* almond milk?

Manufacturers are heeding the call of consumers and creating a wide variety of almond milk options. Flavored almond milks include vanilla and chocolate as well as others. Here are some of the many types of almond milks you can find on your grocer's shelf or in the refrigerator case:

- plain (sweetened, no added flavorings)
- reduced sugar (lightly sweetened)
- unsweetened plain (no added sugar or flavorings)
- unsweetened flavored (no added sugar)

The Advantages of Almond Milk

Just like the mighty almond, almond milk is high in protective antioxidants, particularly vitamin E, and rich in flavonoids. Unlike cow's milk, almond milk contains no cholesterol and no saturated fats, so it won't damage the cardiovascular system.

Just one cup of almond milk also includes significant amounts of magnesium, manganese, selenium, and vitamin E. Magnesium helps to break down the food we eat into energy; in addition, it supports the parathyroid glands, which produce hormones that promote good bone health. Manganese activates enzymes that aid digestion; it's also important for strong teeth and bones. Selenium helps fight illness by supporting the immune system. And with the power of vitamin E, almond milk fights free radicals, which are responsible for the effects of aging.

Almond milk has the highest concentrations of vitamins and minerals compared to soy and rice milks. While dairy milk and commercial nondairy milks are often fortified with various vitamins and minerals, almond milk comes by most of these nutrients naturally. This means that homemade almond milk is just as nutritious as any commercial almond milk found in stores, and even better, it will be free of preservatives, additives, and thickeners.

> Almonds are one of the best sources of the antioxidant vitamin E. One ounce of almonds provides 35 percent of the Daily Value.

Almond milk is the ideal alternative to dairy milk, especially for people who are trying to lower their fat and calorie intakes. Depending on the water-to-nut ratio used, a serving of unsweetened almond milk (about 1 cup) has only 40 calories, 1 gram of fiber, and about 3 grams of heart-healthy fats.

Because almond milk contains no animal products or by-products, it's suitable for vegans and vegetarians. Plus, it's naturally free of gluten, lactose, and casein, making it the perfect option for people who are sensitive to gluten or dairy products.

Milking the Mighty Almond

Although packaged almond milk is readily available, it's easy and inexpensive to make spectacular almond milk at home too. In doing so, you can take advantage of almond milk's impressive nutritional content and culinary versatility, while making the milk as rich or sweet as you want it to be and in all your favorite flavors.

Making fresh, homemade almond milk is surprisingly fast and simple, and minimal equipment is needed: just a blender and a nut milk bag. For the initial processing, a powerful, high-speed blender (such as a Vitamix or Blendtec) is certainly advantageous, as it will do a superior job of grinding the almonds very finely. However, even the average home blender will perform satisfactorily. A nut milk bag (also called a sprout bag) is nothing more complicated than an inexpensive, sturdy, fine-mesh bag that is used to strain out the ground nut particles from freshly processed nut milk. If you don't have a nut milk bag (although I highly recommend purchasing one), you can use a fine-mesh strainer lined with a double layer of ordinary cheesecloth instead.

The most time-consuming aspect of making fresh almond milk is soaking the whole, raw, natural almonds in water for eight to twelve hours. Fortunately, the almonds do all the hard work; all you have to do is plan ahead.

Although soaking is technically optional, it's not a step you should skip. Soaking almonds not only helps plump and soften them so they'll blend more easily, there are important health benefits associated with soaking nuts. Almonds, like other nuts, naturally contain phytic acid. When foods containing phytic acid are consumed without prior soaking, the phytic acid binds to minerals in the intestinal tract and can lead to mineral deficiencies. Soaking helps to break down the phytic acid and makes almonds (and almond milk) more digestible. Always drain and discard the soaking water and rinse the almonds well before using them to make milk.

In the next chapter of this book, I offer recipes for homemade almond milk in both basic and rich versions. In subsequent recipes, whenever one type is preferable for the best results, I recommend it in the ingredient list. As daunting as making almond milk from scratch may seem to cooks who have never done it, the process is surprisingly easy, fun, and cost-effective, and the results are utterly delicious.

The Almond Dairy

CHAPTER

2

basic almond milk

MAKES 4 CUPS

As convenient as it may seem to simply buy packaged almond milk, it's quick, easy, and more cost-effective to make your own. Here is a simple recipe for basic, everyday almond milk that you can enjoy for drinking, cooking, and baking.

> 1¼ cups **natural almonds,** soaked in water 8 to 12 hours, drained, and rinsed
>
> 4 cups **water**

Put the almonds and water in a blender and process on high speed until smooth. Strain the mixture through a nut milk bag and into a large bowl. Secure the top of the bag and squeeze as much liquid as possible from the mixture, starting at the top of the bag and working your way down. When all the milk has been expressed, pour it into a clean glass jar or bottle, cover tightly, and refrigerate until ready to use. Stored in the refrigerator, the milk will keep for 4 days. If some separation occurs, simply shake well to homogenize it before using.

SWEET ALMOND MILK: Add 2 to 4 pitted medjool dates to the blender before processing. Alternatively, stir in your favorite sweetener to taste after the milk has been strained.

Per cup: 263 calories, 10 g protein, 23 g fat (2 g sat), 6 g carbohydrates, 0 mg sodium, 187 mg calcium, 5 g fiber
Note: Analysis is based on the nutritional content of the almonds prior to straining.

rich almond milk

MAKES 4 CUPS

This rich, full-bodied almond milk has a delectable flavor and a creamy mouthfeel. It's a suitable alternative to use in almost any recipe that calls for dairy milk.

> 2 cups **natural almonds,** soaked in water 8 to 12 hours, drained, and rinsed
>
> 4 cups **water**

Put the almonds and water in a blender and process on high speed until smooth. Strain the mixture through a nut milk bag and into a large bowl. Secure the top of the bag and squeeze as much liquid as possible from the mixture, starting at the top of the bag and working your way down. When all the milk has been expressed, pour it into a clean glass jar or bottle, cover tightly, and refrigerate until ready to use. Stored in the refrigerator, the milk will keep for 4 days. If some separation occurs, simply shake well to homogenize it before using.

The earliest varieties of almonds were found in China, carried by traders down the ancient silk road to Greece, Turkey, and the Middle East.

Per cup: 420 calories, 16 g protein, 36 g fat (3 g sat), 10 g carbohydrates, 0 mg sodium, 300 mg calcium, 8 g fiber

Note: Analysis is based on the nutritional content of the almonds prior to straining.

almond cream

Almond milk tends to break apart when boiled down, especially if it's reduced to be as thick as dairy cream. The solution? Almond cream! Use this rich, plant-based alternative as a garnish for soups, an enrichment for sauces, or a base for salad dressings.

> 1 cup **blanched almonds, soaked in water 8 to 12 hours, drained, and rinsed**
>
> 1 cup **water**

Put the almonds and water in a blender and process on high speed until smooth. Strain through a fine-mesh sieve. Scrape into a clean glass jar, seal tightly, and refrigerate until ready to use. Stored in the refrigerator, the cream will keep for 4 days.

TIP Blanched almonds will produce a beautiful white cream. If the color of the cream isn't important for the dish you'll be using it in, feel free to substitute natural almonds.

HERB CREAM: After the mixture is strained, return it to the blender and add 1 cup of fresh herbs (such as basil, cilantro, lemon verbena, mint, or oregano), firmly packed, and process on high speed until smooth. Strain through a fine-mesh sieve. Scrape into a clean glass jar, seal tightly, and refrigerate until ready to use. Stored in the refrigerator, the cream will keep for 4 days.

Per ¼ cup: 210 calories, 8 g protein, 18 g fat (1 g sat), 5 g carbohydrates, 0 mg sodium, 150 mg calcium, 4 g fiber
Note: Analysis is based on the nutritional content of the almonds prior to straining.

basic white sauce

MAKES 1 CUP

Long before it was common to thicken sauces by reduction, béchamel was the mother sauce of French cooking. The original version of this sauce, *balsamella,* is used in Italian cuisine. This basic white sauce can be used as an ingredient in casseroles, soups, gravies, and other sauces. It can also serve as a thickener or binder in other recipes.

> 2 tablespoons **vegan butter**
> 2 tablespoons unbleached all-purpose **white flour**
> 1 cup **unsweetened almond milk** or Rich Almond Milk (page 10)
> ⅛ teaspoon **sea salt**
> ⅛ teaspoon freshly grated **nutmeg** or ground nutmeg
> Freshly ground **black pepper**

Put the butter in a small saucepan over medium heat. When the butter is melted, add the flour and cook, whisking constantly, until just before it begins to brown, 1½ to 2 minutes. Whisk in the almond milk. Cook, whisking constantly, until the mixture thickens, about 1 minute. Stir in the salt and nutmeg and season with pepper to taste.

Per ½ cup: 148 calories, 1 g protein, 13 g fat (4 g sat), 7 g carbohydrates, 225 mg sodium, 150 mg calcium, 1 g fiber
Note: Analysis doesn't include freshly ground black pepper to taste.

roasted pepper cream

MAKES 2 CUPS

Roasted peppers and almond cream are a delightful match, enhanced further in this sauce with the addition of garlic, cayenne, and smoked paprika. Spoon this sauce over pasta or grilled vegetables, or put it in an attractive bowl and pass it at the table as a condiment.

- 2 roasted **red bell peppers** (see tip)
- 1 cup **blanched almonds,** soaked in water 8 to 12 hours, drained, and rinsed
- ¾ cup **water,** plus more as needed
- 1 clove **garlic**
- ½ teaspoon **smoked paprika**
- ¼ teaspoon **cayenne**
- ¼ teaspoon **sea salt**

  Pinch **saffron** (optional)

Put the bell peppers, almonds, water, garlic, paprika, cayenne, salt, and optional saffron in a blender and process on high speed until smooth. Strain through a fine-mesh sieve. If the mixture seems too thick, stir in a little water, 1 teaspoon at a time, to make a thick, creamy sauce. Use at once or transfer to a jar, seal tightly, and store in the refrigerator for up to 4 days.

 Jarred roasted bell peppers make this recipe a cinch to prepare.

Per ½ cup: 215 calories, 8 g protein, 18 g fat (1 g sat), 8 g carbohydrates, 152 mg sodium, 81 mg calcium, 4 g fiber

caramelized onion cream

MAKES 1 CUP

Caramelizing onions mellows their oniony taste, giving the vegetable a uniquely elegant flavor. The combination of caramelized onions and almond cream creates an exquisite topping for any dish that garlic would overwhelm. Try it atop Mashed Potatoes (page 104) or grilled vegetables, tofu, or tempeh.

> 1 cup finely diced **onion**
> ⅓ cup **coconut oil**
> ¼ teaspoon **sea salt**, plus more as needed
> ¾ cup **Almond Cream** (page 11)
> 1 teaspoon chopped **fresh parsley**
> Freshly ground **black pepper**

Put the onion and oil in a small saucepan over medium-high heat and swirl until the oil is melted. Decrease the heat to medium-low and cook, stirring frequently, until the onion is brown all over, about 15 minutes. Continue cooking, stirring constantly, until the onion has turned light brown all over, about 5 minutes longer. Remove from the heat and immediately transfer to a small bowl. The onion will continue to brown as the oil cools. Add the salt and stir several times while the onion and oil are cooling.

Set a strainer over a small bowl. When the onion is completely cool, pour the oil and onion into the strainer. Transfer the onion and 2 teaspoons of the oil to a medium bowl. Reserve the remaining oil for another use (it will be rich and flavorful). Add the Almond Cream and parsley and stir until well combined. Season with pepper and additional salt to taste. Use at once or transfer to a jar, seal tightly, and store in the refrigerator for up to 4 days.

TIP If you intend to use Caramelized Onion Cream in another dish, take care not to add too much salt, since there may already be salt in the other dish.

chef's note: Caramelization is the process of transforming sugar into caramel through sustained heat, which creates a dramatically enhanced flavor profile. The sugars in any fruit or vegetable will caramelize when heated this way, which is what gives them such an attractive browned color, flavor, and aroma.

Per ¼ cup: 345 calories, 7 g protein, 33 g fat (16 g sat), 8 g carbohydrates, 142 mg sodium, 127 mg calcium, 4 g fiber

Note: Analysis doesn't include freshly ground black pepper to taste; analysis for the Almond Cream in this recipe is based on the almonds prior to straining.

browned garlic cream

MAKES 1 CUP

Lightly browned garlic has a unique, addictive flavor that makes it ideal for enhancing virtually any savory dish. When it's folded into almond cream, as it is in this recipe, the garlic bite is mollified, and the cream helps the flavor melt into anything it touches. This sauce is heavenly as a topping for baked potatoes or simply spread on toast.

½ cup **garlic cloves**, peeled and cut in half lengthwise

⅓ cup **coconut oil**

¼ teaspoon **sea salt**

¾ cup **Almond Cream** (page 11)

Put the garlic and oil in a small saucepan over medium-high heat and swirl until the oil is melted. Tip the pan so that the oil and garlic are gathered against one side, and swirl gently to keep the garlic moving constantly. When the garlic has turned light tan, remove from the heat and immediately transfer to a small bowl. The garlic will continue to brown as the oil cools. Add the salt and stir several times while the garlic and oil are cooling.

Set a strainer over a small bowl. When the garlic is completely cool, pour the oil and garlic into the strainer. Transfer the garlic to a cutting board and reserve the oil for another use (it will be rich and flavorful).

Chop and mash the garlic into a smooth paste. Transfer the paste to a medium bowl, add the Almond Cream, and stir until well combined. Use at once or transfer to a jar, seal tightly, and store in the refrigerator for up to 4 days.

Per ¼ cup: 333 calories, 7 g protein, 30 g fat (15 g sat), 9 g carbohydrates, 143 mg sodium, 129 mg calcium, 3 g fiber

Note: Analysis for the Almond Cream in this recipe is based on the almonds prior to straining.

almond crema

MAKES 2 CUPS

Crema is the Spanish word for "cream," but as an English culinary term, it refers to the thin, slightly sour cream that's ubiquitous in Mexican cuisine. It's also similar to the French *crème fraîche.* Use Almond Crema in place of dairy sour cream or mayonnaise, or try it as a topping for grilled vegetables or your favorite Mexican and French dishes.

1 cup **blanched almonds,** soaked in water 8 to 12 hours, drained, and rinsed

1 cup **water**

3 tablespoons freshly squeezed **lime juice**

¼ teaspoon **sea salt**

Put all the ingredients in a blender and process on high speed until smooth. Strain through a fine-mesh sieve. If the mixture seems thick, add a little additional water, 1 teaspoon at a time, to make a slightly runny cream.

Calcium-rich almonds are a good choice to ensure you're getting enough of this bone-building mineral.

Per ¼ cup: 106 calories, 4 g protein, 9 g fat (1 g sat), 3 g carbohydrates, 70 mg sodium, 76 mg calcium, 2 g fiber

Note: Analysis is based on the nutritional content of the almonds prior to straining.

chile ancho crema

MAKES 1½ CUPS

There are dozens of unique chiles used in Mexican cuisine but none quite as popular as the ancho, in part because it packs more flavor than heat. This *crema* makes a zesty sandwich spread and is terrific as a topping for corn on the cob and baked potatoes.

> 2 large **dried ancho chiles**, soaked in hot water 1 to 2 hours and drained
>
> 1 cup **blanched almonds**, soaked 8 to 12 hours, drained, and rinsed
>
> 2 tablespoons freshly squeezed **lime juice**
>
> 2 cloves **garlic**, peeled
>
> ¼ teaspoon **sea salt**

Slit the side of each chile with a paring knife and remove the seeds and stem. Put the chiles in a blender along with the almonds, lime juice, garlic, and salt. Process on high speed until smooth. If the mixture seems thick, add a little water, 1 teaspoon at a time, to make a slightly runny cream.

CHILE CHIPOTLE CREMA: Replace the ancho chiles with 2 canned chipotles en adobo and add ½ cup of water. Chipotle chiles are jalapeño chiles that have ripened on the bush until they turn red; they are then dried and smoked. Much hotter than their cousin, the ancho chile, their robust, inimitable flavor is unparalleled.

chef's note: When poblano chiles are allowed to ripen on the bush until they turn red and then are dried, they are called *chiles anchos*, or "wide chiles," presumably because they become slightly flattened in the process. What is not noted in the name is the way that the drying process dramatically enhances their flavor, even when they're reconstituted in water.

Per ¼ cup: 152 calories, 6 g protein, 13 g fat (1 g sat), 7 g carbohydrates, 102 mg sodium, 6 mg calcium, 3 g fiber

Drink Up!

vanilla-date smoothie 20
blueberry-almond smoothie 21
goji-grape smoothie 22
lemon-pomegranate smoothie 23
fig smoothie with mint 24
ginger-pear smoothie 25
orange-ginger smoothie 26
matcha-mint smoothie 27
green breakfast smoothie 28

chocolate-tangerine smoothie 29
chocolate-raspberry smoothie 30
cherry shake 31
chai 32
cappuccino 33
hot chocolate 34
dark-chocolate milk 35
healthy and heavenly
chocolate milk 36

vanilla-date smoothie

MAKES 1 SERVING

Despite its ease and simplicity, this drink is both richly satisfying and healthful. The dates meld with the vanilla flavor, making it perfectly sweet without added sugar.

- 1 cup plain or vanilla **almond milk** or Rich Almond Milk (page 10)
- 1 frozen medium **banana,** broken into chunks (optional; see tip)
- 2 pitted **medjool dates**
- ½ **vanilla bean,** chopped, or 1 teaspoon vanilla extract

Put all the ingredients in a blender and process on high speed until smooth. Serve at once.

TIP Although using a frozen banana in smoothies is entirely optional, including it will add more body, substance, and creaminess.

Per serving: 297 calories, 2 g protein, 3 g fat (0.1 g sat), 69 g carbohydrates, 161 mg sodium, 476 mg calcium, 7 g fiber

blueberry-almond smoothie

MAKES 1 SERVING

Packed with healthful antioxidants, this naturally sweet beverage is incredibly quick and easy to prepare, and the flavor will transport you to a world beyond.

- 1 cup plain **almond milk** or Rich Almond Milk (page 10)
- 1 frozen medium **banana, broken into chunks** (optional; see tip, page 20)
- ⅓ cup frozen **blueberries**
- 2 **medjool dates,** pitted
- ¼ teaspoon **almond extract**

Put all the ingredients in a blender and process on high speed until smooth. Serve at once.

> Because of the exceptionally healthy fatty-acid profile of almonds, in concert with their high fiber content, diets featuring almonds can help to suppress appetite and may actually promote weight loss.

Per serving: 324 calories, 3 g protein, 3 g fat (0.1 g sat), 76 g carbohydrates, 161 mg sodium, 479 mg calcium, 8 g fiber

goji-grape smoothie

MAKES 1 SERVING

Goji berries earned the nickname "red diamonds" because of their unusually high nutrient content. Grapes are rich in anthocyanins, the antioxidants found in red and purple fruits. These two superfoods are blended with healthy almond milk in this tasty smoothie to make one power-packed way to start the day.

1 cup plain **almond milk** or Rich Almond Milk (page 10)

1 frozen medium **banana,** broken into chunks (optional; see tip, page 20)

¼ cup frozen **grape juice concentrate**

2 tablespoons dried **goji berries,** soaked in warm water 10 minutes to soften and drained

2 pitted **medjool dates**

Put all the ingredients in a blender and process on high speed until smooth. Serve at once.

GOJI-AÇAÍ SMOOTHIE: Replace the frozen grape juice concentrate with frozen açaí purée. Açaí berries have the highest concentration of anthocyanins of all fruits, including grapes.

chef's note: Goji berries, also called wolfberries, are characterized by their bright orange-red color and raisin-like shape. They are one amazing superfood, packing all nine essential amino acids, high levels of vitamin C, calcium, fiber, iron, selenium, twenty-one trace minerals, and the highest concentration of carotenoids of any food.

Per serving: 516 calories, 6 g protein, 4 g fat (0.1 g sat), 124 g carbohydrates, 156 mg sodium, 487 mg calcium, 10 g fiber

lemon-pomegranate smoothie

MAKES 1 SERVING

Pomegranates contain a powerful antioxidant called punicalagin, which is credited with lowering cholesterol and blood pressure and helping to keep arteries clear. Oh—and they're also delicious!

> 1 cup plain **almond milk** or Basic or Sweet Almond Milk (page 9)
>
> 1 frozen medium **banana,** broken into chunks (optional; see tip, page 20)
>
> ⅓ cup **pomegranate seeds**
>
> 2 **medjool dates,** pitted
>
> Grated zest of 1 **lemon**

Put all the ingredients in a blender and process on high speed until smooth. Serve at once.

Per serving: 346 calories, 3 g protein, 4 g fat (0.1 g sat), 82 g carbohydrates, 154 mg sodium, 493 mg calcium, 9 g fiber

fig smoothie with mint

MAKES 1 SERVING

Figs are high in fiber, potassium, and vitamin B$_6$, all of which bode well for general health. The mint in this smoothie adds a refreshing, irresistible layer of flavor along with beautiful specks of color. Your body will be singing as you drink this.

- 1 cup plain **almond milk** or Basic or Sweet Almond Milk (page 9)
- 1 frozen medium **banana,** broken into chunks (optional; see tip, page 20)
- 3 dried black **Mission figs,** soaked in water 10 minutes to soften, drained, and coarsely chopped (see tip)
- 2 pitted **medjool dates**
- ½ teaspoon **vanilla extract**
- 12 fresh **mint leaves**

Put the almond milk, optional banana, figs, dates, and vanilla extract in a blender and process on high speed until smooth. Add the mint and pulse just until finely chopped. Serve at once.

TIP If you have access to fresh black Mission or brown Turkey figs, feel free to use them instead of the dried figs. No soaking is necessary.

Per serving: 384 calories, 3 g protein, 3 g fat (0.1 g sat), 89 g carbohydrates, 167 mg sodium, 521 mg calcium, 12 g fiber

ginger-pear smoothie

MAKES 1 SERVING

Ginger, one of nature's most potent healing foods, marries beautifully with pears, especially in a creamy drink like this one.

- 1 cup plain **almond milk** or Basic or Sweet Almond Milk (page 9)
- 1 frozen medium **banana,** broken into chunks (optional; see tip, page 20)
- ½ ripe Bartlett or Anjou **pear,** coarsely chopped
- 2 **medjool dates,** pitted
- 1 teaspoon peeled and chopped or grated fresh **ginger**
- ¼ teaspoon **vanilla extract** (optional)

Put all the ingredients in a blender and process on high speed until smooth. Serve at once.

NUTRITION IN HOMEMADE ALMOND MILK

It's difficult to calculate a broad nutritional breakdown of unsweetened homemade almond milk, because there are many variables, such as the almond-to-water ratio used, how much of the pulp remains, and how much liquid remains in the pulp. Commercial products contain more water than fresh almond milk, so their nutritional breakdowns aren't comparable to homemade. Those products also typically include oils, sugars, and other additives that fresh, homemade products don't.

Per serving: 355 calories, 2 g protein, 3 g fat (0.1 g sat), 88 g carbohydrates, 162 mg sodium, 481 mg calcium, 10 g fiber

orange-ginger smoothie

MAKES 1 SERVING

This smoothie makes an excellent light breakfast. It's loaded with both flavor and essential nutrients, including potassium, protein, and vitamin C.

2 **oranges**

1 cup plain **almond milk** or Basic or Sweet Almond Milk (page 9), **plus more as needed**

1 frozen medium **banana, broken into chunks** (optional; see tip, page 20)

½ cup **hemp seeds** (optional)

4 pitted **medjool dates**

2 teaspoons peeled and chopped fresh **ginger**

Grate the zest off the oranges directly into a blender (see note). Squeeze the oranges and pour the juice into the blender. Add the almond milk, optional banana, optional hemp seeds, dates, and ginger. Process on high speed until smooth. If the mixture seems too thick, add a little more almond milk and process again. Serve at once.

chef's note: Use a Microplane grater for the best results when removing the zest from citrus fruits. If you don't have a Microplane grater, you can use the fine side of a box grater or a vegetable peeler to carefully remove just the flavorful colored layer of zest, avoiding the bitter white pith.

Per serving: 574 calories, 7 g protein, 4 g fat (0.2 g sat), 143 g carbohydrates, 155 mg sodium, 638 mg calcium, 17 g fiber

matcha-mint smoothie

MAKES 1 SERVING

Matcha, which is dried and ground Japanese green tea, is an antioxidant powerhouse. Mint is very beneficial to digestion and provides a pleasant counterpoint to matcha's characteristic astringency. Together, they're a matcha made in heaven.

> 1 cup plain **almond milk** or Basic or Sweet Almond Milk (page 9)
>
> 1 frozen medium **banana, broken into chunks** (optional; see tip, page 20)
>
> ½ cup **hemp seeds** (optional)
>
> ¼ cup fresh **mint leaves,** firmly packed
>
> 4 **medjool dates,** pitted
>
> 1 tablespoon **matcha**

Put all the ingredients in a blender and process on high speed until smooth. Serve at once.

chef's note: Matcha is dried and finely milled Japanese green tea with the unique quality of being both stimulating and relaxing. These dual properties are what made it ideal for Japanese warriors and meditative monks alike, as each group valued alertness and centered calm. A daily dose of matcha can boost your energy throughout the day, without the jitters of standard caffeinated beverages. In addition, matcha is high in chlorophyll, which gives the tea its signature color and helps build red blood cells. It's also abundant in antioxidants, along with chromium, magnesium, selenium, zinc, and vitamin C.

Per serving: 487 calories, 8 g protein, 3 g fat (0.1 g sat), 115 g carbohydrates, 161 mg sodium, 617 mg calcium, 16 g fiber

green breakfast smoothie

MAKES 2 SERVINGS

The alkalizing effect of the fresh green fruits and vegetables in this gorgeous green smoothie is nothing short of miraculous. There's no better way to start the day.

1½ cups plain **almond milk** or Basic or Sweet Almond Milk (page 9), **plus more as needed**

1 frozen medium **banana,** broken into chunks (optional; see tip, page 10)

1 cup stemmed and coarsely chopped **Tuscan kale,** firmly packed

1 **kiwi,** peeled

½ Granny Smith or other tart **green apple,** cored

¼ cup fresh **mint leaves,** firmly packed

2 pitted **medjool dates**

1 tablespoon freshly squeezed **lime juice**

Put all the ingredients in a blender and process on high speed until smooth. If the mixture is too thick, add more almond milk as needed to achieve the desired consistency and process again. Serve at once.

Per serving: 244 calories, 4 g protein, 2 g fat (0.1 g sat), 58 g carbohydrates, 93 mg sodium, 315 mg calcium, 8 g fiber

chocolate-tangerine smoothie

MAKES 2 SERVINGS

Chocolate and sweet citrus are a classic combination, most frequently appearing in cakes and confections. This smoothie is a delightful and unusual way to fuse these two delectable flavors.

- 2 **tangerines** or **tangelos**
- 1½ cups plain **almond milk** or Basic or Sweet Almond Milk (page 9)
- 1 frozen medium **banana,** broken into chunks (optional; see tip, page 20)
- 4 tablespoons **unsweetened cocoa powder**
- 4 **medjool dates,** pitted

Grate the tangerine zest directly into a blender (see chef's note, page 26). Remove and discard the remaining peel. Break up the fruit into several pieces, remove the seeds, and put the fruit in the blender. Add the almond milk, optional banana, cocoa powder, and dates. Process on high speed until smooth. Serve at once.

chef's note: When they're available, reach for satsuma tangerines instead of regular tangerines or tangelos. Satsumas, a seedless variety of mandarin, have a unique flavor. They are also quite sweet and very easy to peel. You can use almost the entire fruit, and you'll benefit from the bioflavonoids found in the fruit's membranes. Whenever possible, use the satsuma's flavor-rich zest in recipes. Satsumas are seasonal, however, coming out in late fall to early winter. If they aren't available, tangerines or tangelos make excellent substitutes (just be sure to remove their seeds before using).

Per serving: 300 calories, 5 g protein, 4 g fat (1 g sat), 73 g carbohydrates, 117 mg sodium, 416 mg calcium, 11 g fiber

chocolate-raspberry smoothie

For something so effortless to whip together, this smoothie evokes the elegance of a time-consuming classic dessert.

- 1½ cups plain **almond milk** or Basic or Sweet Almond Milk (page 9)
- 1 frozen medium **banana, broken into chunks** (optional; see tip, page 20)
- 1 cup frozen **raspberries**
- ¼ cup **unsweetened cocoa powder**
- 7 pitted **medjool dates**
- 1 tablespoon **coconut oil**
- ½ **vanilla bean**, chopped, or 1 teaspoon vanilla extract

Put all the ingredients in a blender and process on high speed until smooth. Serve at once.

Per serving: 445 calories, 6 g protein, 11 g fat (7 g sat), 96 g carbohydrates, 117 mg sodium, 423 mg calcium, 16 g fiber

cherry shake

MAKES 4 SERVINGS

This shake has the flavor and mouthfeel of an over-the-top indulgence (think ice cream), but it's an illusion. All the ingredients are healthy whole foods. On the other hand, why should healthy and indulgent be mutually exclusive?

- 2 cups fresh or thawed frozen pitted **cherries**
- 2 cups plain **almond milk** or Basic or Sweet Almond Milk (page 9)
- 9 pitted **medjool dates**
- ½ **vanilla bean**, chopped, or 1 teaspoon vanilla extract

Put all the ingredients in a blender and process on high speed until smooth. Serve at once.

> The almond is botanically a stone fruit related to the cherry, peach, and plum.

Per serving: 223 calories, 2 g protein, 1 g fat (0 g sat), 56 g carbohydrates, 76 mg sodium, 270 mg calcium, 6 g fiber

chai

In the vast, sophisticated world that is Indian cuisine, nothing is as quick or accessible as a simple cup of chai, the spiced tea known and loved in coffee shops everywhere. There are packaged formulas and concentrates, but they don't hold a candle to this flavorful homemade version made with almond milk.

    1 cup **water**
    ¼ cup chopped or grated fresh **ginger**
    1 **cinnamon stick**
    7 **cardamom seeds**, crushed
    4 **cloves**
    4 teaspoons **black tea**
    2 cups plain **almond milk** or Basic or Sweet Almond Milk
      (page 9)
      Sweetener

Put the water, ginger, cinnamon stick, cardamom, and cloves in a small saucepan and bring to a boil over high heat. Decrease the heat to medium and simmer for 10 minutes. Remove from the heat and add the tea. Let steep for 3 minutes; for an even stronger tea, steep for 6 minutes. Strain the tea and return to the saucepan. Stir in the almond milk and heat over low heat. Stir in sweetener to taste. Serve at once.

Per serving: 74 calories, 1 g protein, 3 g fat (0 g sat), 11 g carbohydrates, 163 mg sodium, 450 mg calcium, 1 g fiber
Note: Analysis doesn't include sweetener to taste.

cappuccino

Homemade, dairy-free cappuccino is not identical to what you can get at the coffee bar, but it's just as delicious. This popular Italian breakfast drink, topped with foamed milk, dates back to the early twentieth century, but the name wasn't associated with the beverage until shortly before 1950. Once the espresso is made, the rest is very easy.

> 1 cup plain **almond milk,** Rich Almond Milk (page 10), **or** Sweet Almond Milk (page 9)
>
> 3 shots freshly pressed **espresso coffee** (see chef's note)
> **Powdered chocolate,** for dusting
> **Sweetener**

Put the almond milk in a small saucepan and heat over high heat, whisking vigorously and constantly. As the milk begins to foam, pay close attention; don't let it boil, or the foam will collapse. As soon as the milk is hot and foamy, remove from the heat. Quickly pour the espresso into two warmed coffee cups. Pour the hot foamed milk over the coffee, dividing it equally. Dust the tops with powdered chocolate. Serve at once, with sweetener on the side to add as desired.

chef's note: There are three ways to prepare espresso coffee: (1) traditionally, with an espresso machine, (2) semi-traditionally, in a stovetop espresso pot, and (3) heretically, in a French press. Obtain your tool of choice and you'll be well on your way to fabulous almond-milk cappuccino.

Per serving: 31 calories, 1 g protein, 2 g fat (0.3 g sat), 2 g carbohydrates, 66 mg sodium, 151 mg calcium, 1 g fiber
Note: Analysis doesn't include powdered chocolate for dusting or sweetener to taste.

hot chocolate

On a cold day, nothing hits the spot like a cup of hot chocolate. Most people use only cocoa powder to make this drink, but it's far richer and more gratifying when an ounce or two of dark chocolate has been added.

2 cups plain **almond milk** or Sweet Almond Milk (page 9)

3 tablespoons unsweetened Dutch-processed **cocoa powder**

2 ounces **dark chocolate**

2 tablespoons **maple syrup**

½ teaspoon **vanilla extract**

Sweetener

Put the almond milk and cocoa powder in a small saucepan and heat over medium-high heat, whisking vigorously. When the cocoa powder has dissolved and the milk is hot, decrease the heat to low and add the chocolate. Whisk gently to avoid splashing until the chocolate has melted. Add the maple syrup and vanilla extract and whisk to incorporate. Increase the heat to medium and heat, whisking occasionally, until the mixture reaches the desired temperature. Serve at once, with sweetener on the side to add as desired.

According to Ayurveda, almonds enhance intellect and increase longevity.

Per serving: 266 calories, 4 g protein, 12 g fat (6 g sat), 38 g carbohydrates, 152 mg sodium, 50 mg calcium, 7 g fiber

dark-chocolate milk

MAKES 2 SERVINGS

How to get all the pleasure of chocolate milk without the downside of dairy products? Simple! Just switch to almond milk and proceed as if nothing were out of place.

- 2 cups plain **almond milk,** Rich Almond Milk (page 10), **or** Sweet Almond Milk (page 9)
- 1 tablespoon unsweetened Dutch-processed **cocoa powder**
- ½ ounce **dark chocolate**
- 1 tablespoon **maple syrup**
- ¼ teaspoon **vanilla extract**

Put all the ingredients in a blender and process on high speed until smooth. Refrigerate until cold.

Per serving: 136 calories, 3 g protein, 6 g fat (2 g sat), 21 g carbohydrates, 151 mg sodium, 489 mg calcium, 4 g fiber

healthy and heavenly chocolate milk

MAKES 2 SERVINGS

This is chocolate milk for health-minded adults, but even kids will love it.

  2 cups plain **almond milk**, Rich Almond Milk (page 10), or Sweet Almond Milk (page 9)

  4 **medjool dates**, pitted

  2 tablespoons **unsweetened cocoa powder** or raw cacao powder

  ¼ **vanilla bean**, coarsely chopped, or ¼ teaspoon vanilla extract

Put all the ingredients in a blender and process on high speed until smooth. Refrigerate until cold.

Per serving: 208 calories, 3 g protein, 4 g fat (0 g sat), 47 g carbohydrates, 151 mg sodium, 481 mg calcium, 6 g fiber

Morning Glory

CHAPTER

4

muesli

MAKES 4 SERVINGS

This traditional Swiss breakfast takes just a little foresight, as it needs to be started the night before. It's a very tasty way to kick the day into high gear.

- 1½ cups old-fashioned **rolled oats**
- 1 cup sliced **natural almonds**
- 1 cup unsweetened shredded **dried coconut**
- ½ cup **raw sunflower seeds**
- ½ cup **raw pumpkin seeds**
- ½ cup **dried blueberries**
- ½ cup **raisins**
- 4 cups plain **almond milk** or Basic or Sweet Almond Milk (page 9)
- 2 **apples**, peeled
- 1 cup **raspberries** or sliced **strawberries**

Put the oats, almonds, coconut, sunflower seeds, pumpkin seeds, blueberries, and raisins in a large bowl. Add the almond milk and stir well to combine. Refrigerate for 8 to 12 hours. Just before serving, grate the apples into the bowl, add the raspberries, and stir until evenly distributed.

Per serving: 903 calories, 23 g protein, 56 g fat (23 g sat), 89 g carbohydrates, 253 mg sodium, 836 mg calcium, 16 g fiber

brown rice WITH PINEAPPLE, COCONUT, AND CARDAMOM

MAKES 2 SERVINGS

Leftover brown rice can easily be converted into an unusual breakfast. This recipe is one fine example. An eight-ounce can of pineapple chunks will let you make this dish lickety-split, but if you happen to have a fresh pineapple, so much the better.

- 2 cups cooked **long-grain brown rice**
- 2 cups plain **almond milk** or Basic or Sweet Almond Milk (page 9)
- 1 cup unsweetened shredded **dried coconut**
- 1 teaspoon **cardamom seeds**, crushed
- 1 cup fresh or canned **pineapple chunks** packed in juice, drained if canned

Put the rice, almond milk, coconut, and cardamom in a medium sauce-pan and bring to a boil over medium-high heat. Decrease the heat to medium-low and cook, stirring frequently, until the mixture thickens, about 10 minutes. Remove from the heat and stir in the pineapple. Serve at once.

Almonds have more crunch than any other tree nut.

Per serving: 736 calories, 11 g protein, 40 g fat (32 g sat), 88 g carbohydrates, 180 mg sodium, 470 mg calcium, 15 g fiber

hot buckwheat porridge

WITH APPLE AND DRIED CRANBERRIES

MAKES 1 SERVING

Buckwheat isn't related to wheat; in fact, it's not even a true grain. Instead, it's a gluten-free, pyramid-shaped, grain-like seed related to sorrel and rhubarb. The outer husk of the buckwheat groat is inedible, but the inner fruit is very nutritious, providing all the essential amino acids.

> 3 cups **water**
>
> ⅓ cup toasted **buckwheat groats** (kasha)
>
> ¼ teaspoon **sea salt**
>
> 1 teaspoon **coconut oil**
>
> 1 **apple,** cut into bite-sized pieces (peeling optional)
>
> ¼ teaspoon **ground cinnamon**
>
> 1 cup plain **almond milk** or Basic or Sweet Almond Milk (page 9)
>
> ¼ cup **dried cranberries**
>
> ½ teaspoon **vanilla extract**

Put the water in a medium saucepan and bring to a boil over high heat. Add the buckwheat and salt. Decrease the heat to medium and cook for 7 minutes, stirring occasionally. Drain in a strainer.

Put the oil in a medium saucepan and heat over medium-high heat until melted. Add the apple and cook, stirring almost constantly, until very lightly browned, about 4 minutes. Add the cinnamon and stir for a few seconds. Add the buckwheat, almond milk, cranberries, and vanilla extract. Increase the heat to high and bring to a boil. Decrease the heat to medium and cook, stirring frequently, until thickened, about 5 minutes.

chef's note: First cultivated in Southeast Asia thousands of years ago, buckwheat eventually traveled west and became rooted in Eastern European cuisine, taking center stage in many classic dishes. Buckwheat groats are highly digestible and have a mild flavor, but when they're toasted or roasted, the flavor becomes quite robust. The groats can be cooked like rice and used for salads and side dishes or added to soups and stuffings. Buckwheat can also replace rice or any other grain in casseroles or pilafs.

Per serving: 620 calories, 8 g protein, 10 g fat (4 g sat), 134 g carbohydrates, 719 mg sodium, 468 mg calcium, 14 g fiber

sweet and creamy polenta

MAKES 8 SERVINGS

This creamy, hot, gently sweetened cereal makes a warm, soothing
breakfast or snack or even a dessert after a light meal.

- 1 cup **water**
- ¼ teaspoon ground **vanilla bean**, or ½ teaspoon vanilla extract
- ⅛ teaspoon **sea salt**
- ⅓ cup **polenta**, yellow corn grits, or cornmeal
- ⅔ cup plain **almond milk** or Rich Almond Milk (page 10)
- ¼ cup **toasted almonds**, coarsely chopped
- 1 tablespoon **maple syrup**

Put the water in a small saucepan and bring to a boil over medium-high
heat. Add the salt and polenta, whisking constantly to prevent lumps.
Return to a boil, whisking frequently. Decrease the heat to low and cook,
whisking frequently, until the mixture is thick, about 5 minutes. Add
the almond milk and whisk to combine. Cook, whisking
frequently, until thick and creamy, about 2 minutes. Top
with the almonds and maple syrup and serve at once.

Per serving: 65 calories, 1 g protein, 2 g fat (0 g sat), 9 g carbohydrates, 47 mg sodium, 5 mg calcium, 1 g fiber

blueberry-buckwheat pancakes

MAKES 8 PANCAKES

Blueberries and just a bit of yogurt give these pancakes an extra kick of flavor. Serve them with vegan butter and pure maple syrup or your favorite pancake toppings.

¾ cup unbleached all-purpose **white flour**

½ cup **buckwheat flour**

1 tablespoon **light brown sugar**

¼ teaspoon **sea salt**

1 cup unsweetened **almond milk** or Rich Almond Milk (page 10), **plus more as needed**

4½ teaspoons **Ener-G Egg Replacer** mixed with 6 tablespoons water until frothy

½ cup coconut **yogurt** or soy yogurt

1 tablespoon **vegan butter**, melted

1 teaspoon **vanilla extract**

1 cup fresh **blueberries**

1 tablespoon extra-virgin **coconut oil**

Preheat the oven to 200 degrees F.

Put the white flour, buckwheat flour, sugar, and salt in a medium bowl and whisk to combine.

Put the almond milk, egg-replacer mixture, yogurt, butter, and vanilla extract in a small bowl and whisk to combine. Immediately pour into the flour mixture and stir well to make a pourable batter. If the batter is too thick, whisk in a little more almond milk. Stir in the blueberries.

Heat a smooth griddle or large skillet over medium-high heat. Put 1 teaspoon of the coconut oil on the griddle, spreading it over the surface until melted. For each pancake, pour ⅓ cup of the batter onto the griddle. Repeat for as many pancakes as will fit comfortably on the griddle. Cook for 2 minutes. The pancakes are ready to turn when bubbles appear and burst in the uncooked surface. Turn the pancakes over and cook for 2 minutes on the other side. Transfer to a baking sheet and keep warm in the oven while you cook the remaining pancakes.

Per pancake: 120 calories, 2 g protein, 5 g fat (3 g sat), 19 g carbohydrates, 106 mg sodium, 93 mg calcium, 2 g fiber

almond pulp pancakes

This recipe incorporates both almond milk and the pulp that remains from the milk-making process. The sundered parts are rejoined in a completely new and enchanting form. Top these pancakes with fresh fruit, berries, jam, or whatever else you fancy.

- 1 cup unbleached all-purpose white flour
- ½ cup almond pulp (see page 63)
- 1 tablespoon light brown sugar
- ¼ teaspoon sea salt
- 1½ cups unsweetened almond milk or Rich Almond Milk (page 10), plus more as needed
- 4½ teaspoons Ener-G Egg Replacer mixed with 6 tablespoons water until frothy
- 1 tablespoon vegan butter, melted
- 1 teaspoon almond extract
- ⅓ cup toasted almonds, coarsely chopped (optional)
- 1 tablespoon extra-virgin coconut oil

Preheat the oven to 200 degrees F.

Put the flour, almond pulp, brown sugar, and salt in a medium bowl and whisk to combine.

Put the almond milk, egg-replacer mixture, butter, and almond extract in a small bowl and whisk until well combined. Immediately pour into the flour mixture and stir well to make a pourable batter. If the batter is too thick, whisk in a little more almond milk. Stir in the optional almonds.

Heat a smooth griddle or large skillet over medium-high heat. Put 1 teaspoon of the coconut oil on the griddle, spreading it over the surface until melted. For each pancake, pour ⅓ cup of the batter onto the griddle. Repeat for as many pancakes as will fit comfortably on the griddle. Cook for 2 minutes. The pancakes are ready to turn when bubbles appear and burst in the uncooked surface. Turn the pancakes over and cook for 2 minutes on the other side. Transfer to a baking sheet and keep warm in the oven while you cook the remaining pancakes.

Per pancake: 120 calories, 3 g protein, 6 g fat (2 g sat), 16 g carbohydrates, 105 mg sodium, 9 mg calcium, 1 g fiber

biscuits

MAKES 12 BISCUITS

A basket of warm biscuits with breakfast or with any meal is a most welcome sight.

2 cups unbleached all-purpose **white flour**

1 tablespoon **baking powder**

1 teaspoon **sea salt**

½ cup **vegan butter**, chilled

½ cup unsweetened **almond milk** or Rich Almond Milk (page 10)

1 tablespoon **Ener-G Egg Replacer** mixed with ¼ cup water until frothy

Preheat the oven to 450 degrees F. Line a baking sheet with parchment paper.

Put the flour, baking powder, and salt in a medium bowl and whisk to combine. Cut the butter into tablespoon-sized pieces and pinch them into the flour until only pea-sized pieces remain.

Put the almond milk and egg-replacer mixture in a small bowl and whisk to combine. Pour into the flour mixture and stir until well combined. The mixture will be very dry at first. Knead gently until a dough forms. Transfer the dough to a floured surface and roll out into a rectangle. Fold in thirds, like a letter. Turn the dough a one-quarter turn and roll it out again into a rectangle. Fold again, roll out again, and fold one more time. Roll out to a thickness of about ½ inch. Cut out rounds with a 3-inch biscuit cutter or the open end of a beverage glass and arrange them on the lined baking sheet, spacing them evenly about one-half inch apart. To use the leftover dough, do not knead; instead, stack the pieces and roll them out to ½ inch thick. Cut out as many more rounds as possible.

Bake the biscuits for about 10 minutes, until lightly browned. Serve warm.

Per biscuit: 147 calories, 2 g protein, 7 g fat (2 g sat), 165 g carbohydrates, 342 mg sodium, 31 mg calcium, 1 g fiber

Soups for Every Season

cream of mushroom soup

MAKES 4 SERVINGS

This version of the classic cream soup is far superior to the stuff that comes out of a can, and yet it's surprisingly easy to make and equally as versatile.

6 tablespoons **vegan butter**

1 pound button or cremini **mushrooms,** sliced

¾ cup finely diced **onion**

¾ cup finely diced **celery**

¼ cup chopped fresh **parsley**

3½ cups no-salt-added **vegetable broth**

3 tablespoons unbleached all-purpose **white flour**

1½ cups unsweetened **almond milk** or Rich Almond Milk (page 10)

¼ teaspoon **sea salt**

⅛ teaspoon freshly grated **nutmeg** or ground nutmeg

Freshly ground **black pepper**

Put 3 tablespoons of the butter in a large soup pot over medium-high heat. When the butter is melted, add the mushrooms and cook, stirring frequently, until they are lightly browned, 3 to 5 minutes. Add the onion, celery, and parsley and stir well. Cook until the vegetables are dry and just beginning to stick, about 4 minutes. Stir in the broth and bring to a boil. Decrease the heat to medium and cook, stirring occasionally, for 20 minutes. Transfer to a blender and process on high speed until smooth.

Put the remaining 3 tablespoons of butter in the soup pot over medium-high heat. When the butter is melted, whisk in the flour. Cook, whisking constantly, until the mixture begins to brown, 3 to 4 minutes. Whisk in the almond milk, salt, and nutmeg. Cook, whisking constantly, until the mixture thickens, about 1 minute. Add the mixture from the blender and stir until well combined. Season with pepper to taste. Cook, stirring almost constantly, until hot. Serve at once.

VARIATION: If you prefer a soup with more texture, scoop out about 1 cup of the mushroom mixture with a slotted spoon before processing the remainder in the blender. Stir the mushrooms into the soup after adding the blended mixture to the pot.

Almonds have the same protective flavonoid and antioxidant activity per serving as broccoli and green tea.

Per serving: 256 calories, 6 g protein, 19 g fat (5 g sat), 19 g carbohydrates, 400 mg sodium, 183 mg calcium, 4 g fiber
Note: Analysis doesn't include freshly ground black pepper to taste.

chilled almond soup WITH GARLIC

MAKES 4 SERVINGS

Almost everyone is familiar with traditional red gazpacho, but this cold, tomato-free version, known as *ajo blanco,* was its precursor. In Spain, it's traditional to serve the soup with grapes, either on the side or in the soup.

3	cups crustless day-old **bread cubes**
1½	cups **water**
1	cup **blanched almonds,** soaked in water 8 to 12 hours
1	cup unsweetened **almond milk** or Basic Almond Milk (page 9)
3	cloves **garlic,** halved lengthwise, germ removed (see tip)
½	teaspoon **sea salt**
½	cup extra-virgin **olive oil,** plus more for drizzling
¼	cup **sherry vinegar**
2	tablespoons sliced **natural almonds,** for garnish
1½	cups seedless **green grapes,** for garnish

To make the soup, put the bread cubes, water, blanched almonds, almond milk, garlic, and salt in a blender and process on high speed until very smooth. This could take 2 minutes or longer. With the motor running, pour in the oil and vinegar. Put a fine-mesh sieve over a medium bowl and strain the mixture through it. Cover and refrigerate until cold. This can be done up to 2 days in advance.

To prepare the garnishes, preheat the oven to 400 degrees F. Spread the sliced almonds in a thin layer on a baking sheet and bake them for 5 to 7 minutes, until lightly toasted and browned. Transfer to a cool baking sheet or large plate and let cool completely. Cut the grapes in half lengthwise and put them in a small bowl. Both the toasted almonds and grapes can be prepared up to 1 day in advance.

Garnish each serving of soup with one-quarter of the toasted almonds, placing the almonds in the center of the soup. Drizzle olive oil around the almonds. Serve at once, accompanied by the bowl of the grapes.

TIP The germ is a small sprout in the center of a garlic clove. It's often in the process of turning green, either at the tip or all the way to the root. Because the germ can be bitter and cause indigestion, it's a good idea to remove it.

chef's note: When the Muslims conquered Spain in 711 CE, they brought with them advancements in science, astronomy, mathematics, art, architecture, and of course, cuisine. One dish that had its origins during that time is *sopa de ajo blanco*. Gazpacho came along centuries later, after conquistadores brought tomatoes and peppers back from the New World.

Per serving: 599 calories, 10 g protein, 48 g fat (5 g sat), 15 g carbohydrates, 289 mg sodium, 174 mg calcium, 5 g fiber

Note: Analysis is based on all ingredients prior to straining.

cream of tomato soup

MAKES 4 SERVINGS

This is a simplified version of a classic soup that's easy for anyone to whip up on a whim. If tarragon is in season, you can use a couple of whole sprigs in place of the dried herb; simply remove them just before serving the soup.

- 2 tablespoons **vegan butter**
- 2 tablespoons unbleached all-purpose **white flour**
- 1 cup no-salt-added **vegetable broth** or water
- ¾ cup no-salt-added **tomato paste**
- 1 teaspoon dried **tarragon** (optional)
- 2½ cups unsweetened **almond milk** or Rich Almond Milk (page 10)
- 2½ teaspoons **arrowroot starch**
- 1 tablespoon freshly squeezed **lemon juice**
- ¼ teaspoon **sea salt**
  Freshly ground **black pepper** (optional)

Put the butter in a large pot over medium-high heat. When the butter is melted, add the flour and cook, whisking constantly, until the mixture just begins to color, about 2 minutes. Add the broth, whisking constantly. Cook, whisking constantly, until the mixture thickens, about 1 minute. Add the tomato paste and whisk to combine. Decrease the heat to medium-low and stir in the optional tarragon. Cover and cook, stirring occasionally, for 10 minutes.

Put the almond milk and arrowroot starch in a small bowl and whisk until well combined. Whisk into the soup. Increase the heat to medium-high and bring to a simmer, whisking almost constantly. As soon as the soup thickens, remove from the heat. Add the lemon juice and salt and stir to combine. Season with pepper to taste if desired. Serve at once.

Per serving: 130 calories, 3 g protein, 7 g fat (2 g sat), 14 g carbohydrates, 335 mg sodium, 331 mg calcium, 2 g fiber

carrot soup WITH GINGER AND CARDAMOM

MAKES 4 SERVINGS

This soup is a tantalizing way to enjoy an impressive nutritional punch of beta-carotene and vitamin A. While ginger is a common ingredient in carrot soup, the addition of cardamom and fresh almond milk is a game changer.

 2 tablespoons **coconut oil**

 1 large **onion,** diced

 4 cloves **garlic,** minced

 6 cups grated **carrots**

 ½ teaspoon **sea salt**

 2 cups no-salt-added **vegetable broth**

 2 cups unsweetened **almond milk** or Basic Almond Milk (page 9)

 2 tablespoons peeled and minced fresh **ginger**

 1½ teaspoons crushed **cardamom seeds**

 1 tablespoon snipped fresh **chives,** for garnish

Put the oil in a large soup pot over medium-high heat. When the oil is melted, add the onion and cook, stirring frequently, until the onion is soft, about 5 minutes. Add the garlic and cook, stirring constantly, for 1 minute. Add the carrots and salt and cook, stirring constantly, until almost dry, about 4 minutes. Add the broth and stir until well combined. Increase the heat to high and bring to a boil. Decrease the heat to medium and cook, stirring occasionally, until the vegetables are very tender, about 20 minutes.

Transfer the carrot mixture to a blender and rinse out the soup pot. Add the almond milk and ginger to the blender and process on high speed until smooth. Pour the mixture into the pot and heat over medium heat, stirring frequently, until hot. Remove from the heat and stir in the cardamom. Garnish with the chives and serve at once.

Per serving: 174 calories, 3 g protein, 9 g fat (6 g sat), 24 g carbohydrates, 492 mg sodium, 295 mg calcium, 6 g fiber

spiced butternut squash soup

MAKES 4 SERVINGS

There are many versions of spiced butternut squash soup. This very easy one combines Indian and Spanish influences along with almond milk to create a complex flavor profile.

    2 tablespoons **coconut oil**
    2 cups diced **onions**
    6 cups peeled and cubed **butternut squash**
    4 cloves **garlic**, minced
    2 tablespoons ground **coriander**
    2 teaspoons **hot smoked paprika**
    1 teaspoon ground **turmeric**
    ½ teaspoon **sea salt**
    1 cup no-salt-added **vegetable broth** or water
    4 cups unsweetened **almond milk** or Basic Almond Milk
       (page 9)
    ¼ cup chopped fresh **ginger**
    2 tablespoons freshly squeezed **lime juice**

Put the oil in a large soup pot over medium-high heat. When the oil is melted, add the onions and cook, stirring frequently, until the onions are soft, about 5 minutes. Add the squash and garlic and cook, stirring almost constantly, for 2 minutes. Add the coriander, paprika, turmeric, and salt and stir until thoroughly combined and beginning to stick, about 1 minute. Stir in the broth and bring to a boil. Decrease the heat to medium, cover, and cook, stirring occasionally, until the vegetables are tender and the liquid is absorbed, about 20 minutes. Transfer to a blender.

Rinse out the soup pot and put a strainer over it. Add the almond milk and ginger to the blender and process on high speed until smooth. Strain the mixture into the pot. Heat over medium heat, stirring frequently, until hot. Stir in the lime juice and serve at once.

Per serving: 240 calories, 5 g protein, 9 g fat (6 g sat), 41 g carbohydrates, 348 mg sodium, 218 mg calcium, 8 g fiber

fennel and leek soup

MAKES 4 SERVINGS

Fennel is beneficial to digestion, making this soup an excellent first course. Leeks add a welcome secondary layer of flavor, and almond milk deepens and enriches the overall effect.

2 large **fennel bulbs,** with fronds attached

2 **leeks,** white part only

3 tablespoons extra-virgin **olive oil**

3 cups no-salt-added **vegetable broth** or water

½ teaspoon **sea salt**

2 cups unsweetened **almond milk,** Rich Almond Milk (page 10), or Basic Almond Milk (page 9)

⅛ teaspoon freshly ground **black pepper**

Remove the fronds from the fennel stalks and chop the fronds coarsely. Transfer the fronds to a plate, cover, and set aside. Cut the fennel bulbs in half lengthwise, then thinly slice them crosswise. Cut the leeks in half lengthwise and rinse thoroughly under cold running water to remove any grit. Pat them dry and thinly slice crosswise.

Put the oil in a large soup pot over medium-high heat. When the oil is hot, add the sliced fennel and leeks and cook, stirring frequently, until soft and translucent, about 10 minutes. Don't let the vegetables brown. Add the broth and salt and bring to a boil. Decrease the heat to medium and cook, stirring occasionally, until the vegetables are very tender and the liquid is reduced to about 1 cup, about 25 minutes.

Transfer to a blender and add the almond milk and pepper. Reserve about 2 tablespoons of the fennel fronds and add the rest of the fronds to the blender. Process on high speed until smooth. Pour into the pot, straining through a fine-mesh sieve if a smoother soup is desired. Heat over medium heat, stirring frequently, until hot. Garnish with the reserved fennel fronds and serve at once.

Per serving: 180 calories, 3 g protein, 12 g fat (2 g sat), 19 g carbohydrates, 453 mg sodium, 307 mg calcium, 5 g fiber

chile soup with potatoes

MAKES 4 SERVINGS

This soup is creamy, smoky, and spicy. Although it takes a little time to simmer, it pulls together quite quickly.

  3 tablespoons extra-virgin **olive oil**

  1 large **onion,** finely diced

  4 cloves **garlic,** minced

  ½ teaspoon **dried ground chiles** or crushed **red pepper flakes,** or 2 tablespoons dried ground ancho or pasilla chiles

  2 teaspoons **smoked hot paprika**

  ½ teaspoon **sea salt**

  2 russet **potatoes,** peeled and diced

  2 cups no-salt-added **vegetable broth** or water

1½ cups chopped **tomatoes**

  2 cups unsweetened **almond milk** or Basic Almond Milk (page 9)

  ½ cup coarsely chopped fresh **cilantro**

  ¼ cup freshly squeezed **lime juice**

  4 tablespoons **Almond Crema** (page 17; optional)

Put the oil in a large soup pot over medium-high heat. When the oil is hot, add the onion and garlic and stir well. Spread the mixture out to evenly coat the bottom of the pot. Decrease the heat to low, cover, and cook, stirring occasionally and spreading out the mixture again, for 20 minutes. If the mixture is sticking, add 1 tablespoon of water. Do not let the onion and garlic brown. Add the chiles, paprika, and salt and cook, stirring constantly, for 1 minute. Add the potatoes and stir to combine. Increase the heat to medium and cook, stirring frequently, for 3 minutes.

Put the broth and tomatoes in a blender and process on high speed until smooth. Pour into the soup pot and stir well. Increase the heat to high and bring to a boil. Decrease the heat to medium and cook, stirring occasionally, until the potatoes are tender, about 20 minutes. Stir in the almond milk. Scoop out about half the soup, including some of the potatoes, and put in a blender. Process on high speed until smooth. Pour into the pot and heat over medium heat, stirring frequently, until hot.

Just before serving, stir in the cilantro and lime juice. Garnish each bowl of soup with a dollop of the optional crema in the center and serve at once.

Per serving: 289 calories, 9 g protein, 12 g fat (1 g sat), 9 g carbohydrates, 396 mg sodium, 228 mg calcium, 9 g fiber

curried spinach and potato soup

MAKES 4 SERVINGS

Indian spices bring a spark of exotic flavor to any food they touch, even something as non-Indian as a soup like this one. The combination of spinach, potatoes, and almond milk in the soup creates a silky, savory delight.

2	tablespoons **coconut oil**
¼	teaspoon whole **cumin seeds**
1	medium **onion**, finely diced
7	cloves **garlic**, minced
1	tablespoon peeled and grated fresh **ginger**
1	large **tomato**
1	tablespoon **curry powder**
½	teaspoon ground **turmeric**
½	teaspoon **sea salt**
2	medium **russet potatoes**, peeled and diced
1½	pounds **spinach**, stemmed and chopped
3	cups no-salt-added **vegetable broth** or water
3½	cups unsweetened **almond milk**, Rich Almond Milk (page 10), **or** Basic Almond Milk (page 9)
½	cup coarsely chopped fresh **cilantro**, lightly packed
¼	cup freshly squeezed **lime juice**

Put the oil and cumin seeds in a large pot over medium-high heat. Cook, stirring occasionally, until the seeds release their aroma, about 2 minutes. Add the onion, garlic, and ginger and stir well. Spread the mixture out to evenly coat the bottom of the pot. Decrease the heat to low, cover, and cook, stirring occasionally and spreading out the mixture again, for 20 minutes. If the mixture is sticking, add 1 tablespoon of water. Do not let the onion and garlic brown.

Grate the tomato onto a plate and scrape it into the pot. Add the curry powder, turmeric, and salt and stir to combine. Cover and cook, stirring frequently, for 5 minutes. Add the potatoes and stir until evenly coated with the seasonings. Increase the heat to medium-high and cook, stirring constantly, for 2 minutes. If the mixture becomes dry and the potatoes begin to stick, add 2 to 3 tablespoons of water and stir. Add the spinach and stir until well combined. Cook, stirring frequently, for 4 minutes.

Stir in the broth and bring to a boil. Decrease the heat to medium and cook, stirring occasionally, until the vegetables are tender, about 15 minutes. The liquid will reduce and the mixture should be very thick. Transfer about two-thirds of the mixture to a blender. Add the almond milk and process on high speed until smooth. Pour into the pot, add the cilantro and lime juice, and stir until well combined. Heat over medium heat, stirring frequently, until hot. Serve at once.

Per serving: 231 calories, 9 g protein, 11 g fat (6 g sat), 30 g carbohydrates, 591 mg sodium, 697 mg calcium, 7 g fiber

tomato bisque

Perhaps you've encountered a few versions of tomato bisque, from pinkish red to deep vermilion in color and widely varied in flavor. This is a classic recipe, with the only departures being olive oil and thick almond cream as stand-ins for butter and dairy cream.

- 2 tablespoons extra-virgin **olive oil**
- 1 small **onion,** finely diced
- ½ cup peeled and finely diced **carrot**
- ½ cup finely diced **celery**
- 3 cloves **garlic,** minced
- 2 tablespoons unbleached all-purpose **white flour** or other flour
- 2 cups no-salt-added **vegetable broth**
- 3 cups peeled and diced **tomatoes** (see chef's note)
- 3 tablespoons no-salt-added **tomato paste**
- 3 sprigs fresh flat-leaf **parsley**
- 3 sprigs fresh **thyme**
- 1 **bay leaf**
- 1 cup **Almond Cream** (page 11)
  Sea salt
  Freshly ground **black pepper**

Put the oil in a large soup pot over medium-high heat. When the oil is hot, add the onion, carrot, celery, and garlic and cook, stirring constantly, until the mixture is sizzling, about 2 minutes. Decrease the heat to low, cover, and cook, stirring occasionally, for 10 minutes. If the mixture is sticking, add 1 tablespoon of water.

Increase the heat to medium-high, add the flour, and stir vigorously to mix well. Cook, stirring constantly, for 3 minutes. Add the broth, tomatoes, and tomato paste and stir well, making sure to scrape up any bits that may be stuck to the bottom of the pot. Tie the parsley, thyme, and bay leaf into a bundle with kitchen twine and add to the pot. Alternatively, wrap the herbs in cheesecloth and secure with string. Bring the mixture to a boil. Decrease the heat to medium and cook, stirring occasionally, for 30 minutes. Remove and discard the herb bundle.

Transfer the mixture to a blender and add the almond cream. Process on high speed until smooth. Pour into the pot and heat over medium heat, stirring frequently, until hot. Season with salt and pepper to taste. Serve at once.

chef's note: To peel tomatoes, fill a large saucepan with water and bring to a boil over high heat. While the water is coming to a boil, slice a shallow X in the bottom (opposite the stem side) of each tomato with a sharp knife. Fill a bowl with ice water and put it beside the stove.

When the water comes to a boil, add the tomatoes. Boil the tomatoes until the X begins to split open, about 25 seconds. Do not boil longer than 25 to 30 seconds or the tomatoes will soften and cook. Remove the tomatoes from the boiling water using a slotted spoon and immediately put them in the bowl of ice water. Remove the tomatoes from the ice water and peel the skin at the X, pulling the skin back gently with your fingers.

Per serving: 360 calories, 10 g protein, 27 g fat (1 g sat), 21 g carbohydrates, 53 mg sodium, 167 mg calcium, 7 g fiber

Note: Analysis doesn't include sea salt or freshly ground black pepper to taste; analysis for the Almond Cream in this recipe is based on the almonds prior to straining.

eggplant soup

MAKES 4 SERVINGS

Eggplant becomes incredibly succulent in this recipe, due in large part to the slow cooking it receives. Here, the eggplant takes center stage, with onion and garlic playing supporting roles. The result is delightfully light and flavorful.

2 pounds **eggplant**

1 teaspoon **sea salt**, plus more as needed

3 tablespoons extra-virgin **olive oil**

1 large **onion**, finely diced

2 teaspoons minced **garlic**

2 cups no-salt-added **vegetable broth** or water

2 **bay leaves**

3 cups unsweetened **almond milk**, Rich Almond Milk (page 10), **or** Basic Almond Milk (page 9)

Freshly ground **black pepper**

1 tablespoon snipped fresh **chives**, for garnish

Peel the eggplant, cut it into ½-inch dice, and put it in a large bowl. Sprinkle with the salt and toss to distribute it evenly. Put a colander over a large bowl. Transfer the eggplant to the colander and let the bitter juices drain for 30 minutes. Rinse the eggplant under cold running water to remove as much of the salt as possible. Drain well and pat the eggplant dry with a clean tea towel.

Put the oil in a large soup pot over medium-high heat. When the oil is hot, add the onion and cook, stirring constantly, until the onion is warm and aromatic, about 2 minutes. Spread the onion out to evenly coat the bottom of the pot. Decrease the heat to low, cover, and cook, stirring occasionally and spreading out the onion again, for 30 minutes. If the onion is sticking, add 1 tablespoon of water. Do not let the onion brown.

Increase the heat to medium-high, add the eggplant and garlic, and stir until well combined. Continue stirring until the mixture just begins to stick, about 1 minute, then add the broth and bay leaves. Stir well, making sure to scrape up any bits that may have stuck to the bottom of the pot. Bring to a boil. Decrease the heat to medium and cook, stirring occasionally, until the eggplant is tender and almost all the liquid is absorbed, about 20 minutes.

Remove and discard the bay leaves. Transfer about two-thirds of the eggplant mixture to a blender and add the almond milk. Process on high speed until smooth. Pour into the pot and heat over medium heat, stirring constantly, until hot. Season with pepper to taste and additional salt if desired. Garnish with the chives and serve at once.

Almonds are rich in essential minerals, including calcium, iron, magnesium, and zinc.

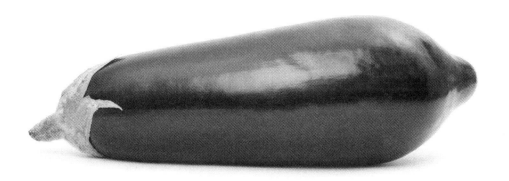

Per serving: 174 calories, 3 g protein, 12 g fat (2 g sat), 16 g carbohydrates, 280 mg sodium, 358 mg calcium, 8 g fiber

Note: Analysis doesn't include freshly ground black pepper to taste.

7

zucchini corn chowder

MAKES 4 SERVINGS

Squash and corn are not only made for each other, but in the American Southwest, they're also often grown together (along with beans). Their flavors and textures meld nicely while magically remaining distinct. This is definitely not the same old corn chowder you might be used to, although it should hit all the familiar notes.

3 tablespoons extra-virgin **olive oil**

1 large **onion**, diced

3 medium **zucchini**, diced

2 small **potatoes, diced** (peeling optional)

2 cloves **garlic**, minced

½ teaspoon **sea salt**

2 cups no-salt-added **vegetable broth** or water

4½ cups fresh or frozen **corn kernels**

3 cups unsweetened **almond milk** or Basic Almond Milk (page 9)

½ teaspoon **hot smoked paprika**, plus more for garnish

1 roasted **red pepper**, diced (see tip, page 13)

8 **scallions**, thinly sliced

Put the oil in a large soup pot over medium-high heat. When the oil is hot, add the onion and cook, stirring frequently, until the onion is soft, about 5 minutes. Add the zucchini, potatoes, garlic, and salt and cook, stirring constantly, until the vegetables begin to stick, about 5 minutes. Add the broth and stir well. Increase the heat to high and bring to a boil. Set aside 2 tablespoons of the corn and add the remainder to the pot. Return to a boil, decrease the heat to medium, and cook, stirring occasionally, until the liquid is absorbed and the vegetables are tender, about 20 minutes. Scoop out about half the vegetables and put them in a blender. Add the almond milk and paprika and process on high speed until smooth. Pour into the pot.

Set aside 2 tablespoons of the roasted red pepper, add the rest to the soup, and stir to combine. Heat over medium heat, stirring frequently, until hot. Set aside 2 tablespoons of the scallions and stir the rest into the hot soup.

Garnish each serving with some of the reserved corn, roasted red pepper, and scallions, and sprinkle with a few pinches of smoked paprika. Serve at once.

WHAT TO DO WITH ALMOND PULP

When you start making fresh almond milk at home, you'll discover that you have an abundance of pulp left behind. There's no need to toss it out or put it in the compost pile. You can put it to good use in very productive and delicious ways:

- Add almond pulp to cereal or a smoothie to boost healthy protein and fiber content.
- Use almond pulp as a replacement for eggs in cookies, muffins, and other baked goods.
- Prepare hummus with almond pulp instead of chickpeas.
- Try almond pulp as the base for a facial mask or scrub.
- Make the following recipes from this book: Almond Pulp Pancakes (page 43), Olive and Herb Crackers (page 113), and Triple-Chocolate Muffins (page 118).

Per serving: 378 calories, 10 g protein, 13 g fat (1 g sat), 58 g carbohydrates, 491 mg sodium, 391 mg calcium, 7 g fiber

kohlrabi cream soup

Kohlrabi is an odd-looking vegetable, resembling a pale green beet with tentacle-like stems that protrude from the sides and grow upward, with lush leaves at the ends. For all its exotic looks, kohlrabi has a very mild flavor, albeit a distinctive one, that stands out best in a cream soup like this one.

1½ pounds **kohlrabi**

2 tablespoons extra-virgin **olive oil**

1½ cups finely diced **onions**

¾ cup finely diced **celery**

¼ teaspoon **sea salt**

2 cups **water**

2 cups unsweetened **almond milk,** Rich Almond Milk (page 10), **or** Basic Almond Milk (page 9), **plus more as needed**

Freshly ground **black pepper**

1 tablespoon snipped **chives,** for garnish

Peel the kohlrabi, taking care to remove all the tough outer layer, and cut it into ¼-inch dice.

Put the oil in a large soup pot over medium-high heat. When the oil is hot, add the onions and celery and stir well. Spread the mixture evenly over the bottom of the pot. Decrease the heat to low, cover, cook, stirring occasionally and spreading out the mixture again, for 15 minutes. If the mixture is sticking, add 1 tablespoon of water. Do not let the vegetables brown.

Add the kohlrabi and salt and stir until well combined. Cook, stirring frequently, for 5 minutes. Stir in the water and bring to a boil. Decrease the heat to medium, cover, and cook, stirring occasionally, until the vegetables are tender and almost all the liquid is absorbed, about 30 minutes. Stir in the almond milk. Increase the heat to medium-high and bring to a boil. Decrease the heat to medium and cook, stirring occasionally, until heated through, about 5 minutes. If the soup is very thick, add a little additional almond milk to thin it slightly. Season with pepper to taste. Garnish with the chives and serve at once.

chef's note: Kohlrabi is the German word for "cabbage turnip." Even though it looks like a root, it's actually a swollen stem that grows over the soil. Kohlrabi is a cruciferous vegetable, belonging to the brassica family, along with broccoli, Brussels sprouts, cabbage, collard greens, and kale. It has an impressive nutritional profile and offers a bounty of health benefits, including abundant antioxidants that can help ward off cancer. Although its flavor is similar to that of a turnip, the kohlrabi is sweeter and milder, and its leaves can be steamed or cooked with oil and garlic, just like spinach and chard.

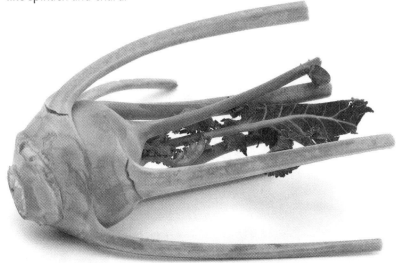

Per serving: 151 calories, 4 g protein, 9 g fat (1 g sat), 17 g carbohydrates, 273 mg sodium, 278 mg calcium, 7 g fiber
Note: Analysis doesn't include freshly ground black pepper to taste.

asparagus soup

MAKES 4 SERVINGS

A popular spring vegetable, prized since ancient times by Greeks and Romans, asparagus is one of the delicacies of the vegetable kingdom. Preparing it in a cream soup is ideal for appreciating both the exquisite flavor and texture of this vegetable at its peak.

2	pounds green **asparagus**
1½	cups finely diced **onions**
⅓	cup no-salt-added **vegetable broth**
3	cups **water**
½	teaspoon **sea salt**
2½	cups unsweetened **almond milk,** Rich Almond Milk (page 10), **or** Basic Almond Milk (page 9)
1	teaspoon **arrowroot starch**
	Freshly ground **black pepper**
1	tablespoon snipped fresh **chives,** for garnish

Break off the woody ends of the asparagus and remove the tough skin from the stems with a vegetable peeler. Cut off the tips about 1 inch down, and set aside. Cut the stems into ½-inch lengths.

Put the onions and broth in a medium soup pot and bring to a boil over medium-high heat. Decrease the heat to medium and cook, stirring occasionally, until the liquid has reduced to about 1 tablespoon, about 30 minutes. Add the asparagus stems, water, and salt and stir to combine. Increase the heat to medium-high and bring to a boil. Decrease the heat to medium, cover, and cook until the stems are very tender, about 25 minutes. The liquid will have reduced to about 2 cups.

While the stems are cooking, fill a small saucepan two-thirds full with lightly salted water and bring to a boil. Add the asparagus tips and cook until tender, about 7 minutes. Drain, refresh under cold running water, and spread the tips out on a clean tea towel to drain thoroughly.

Transfer the asparagus-stem mixture to a blender and add the almond milk and arrowroot starch. Process on high speed until smooth. Pour into the pot, add the asparagus tips, and cook over medium heat, stirring constantly, for 5 minutes. The mixture should have a smooth, light consistency. If it seems too thin, continue to cook, stirring frequently, until it has reduced and thickened slightly. Season with pepper to taste. Garnish with the chives and serve at once.

> The high fiber content of almonds gives them prebiotic properties, which contribute to health in the gastrointestinal tract.

Per serving: 107 calories, 6 g protein, 2 g fat (0.1 g sat), 18 g carbohydrates, 418 mg sodium, 345 mg calcium, 6 g fiber
Note: Analysis doesn't include freshly ground black pepper to taste.

chilled avocado soup

Avocados are naturally creamy, which makes them ideal to use in a chilled, creamy soup. The addition of roasted poblano chiles contributes a hint of the spicy Mexican cuisine in which avocados were likely first used, while the almond milk and chives pull the dish in a decidedly continental direction.

2 **poblano chiles**

3 tablespoons **coconut oil**

2 cups finely diced **onions**

4 teaspoons minced **garlic**

4 cups no-salt-added **vegetable broth** or water

4 ripe **avocados**, cut into small chunks

2 cups unsweetened **almond milk** or Basic Almond Milk (page 9)

¼ cup freshly squeezed **lime juice**

½ teaspoon **sea salt**

1 tablespoon snipped fresh **chives**

Preheat the broiler. Line a baking sheet with foil.

Quarter the chiles lengthwise and remove the seeds and membranes. Arrange the chiles skin-side up on the lined baking sheet. Broil until the skins are evenly blackened. Wrap the chiles in the foil and set aside on the counter for 10 minutes to steam. Remove the foil, put the chiles in a small bowl, and cover with cold water to loosen the skins. Slip off the skins using your fingers and finely dice the chiles.

Put the oil in a medium saucepan over medium heat. When the oil is melted, add the chiles, onions, and garlic, spreading them in an even layer. Decrease the heat to low, cover, and cook until the onions are soft, about 15 minutes. Check occasionally, and if the mixture is sticking, add 1 tablespoon of water. Transfer to a blender and add the broth, avocados, almond milk, lime juice, and salt. Process on high speed until smooth. Pour into a bowl and refrigerate until cold. Garnish with the chives just before serving.

Per serving: 332 calories, 4 g protein, 28 g fat (9 g sat), 24 g carbohydrates, 272 mg sodium, 183 mg calcium, 11 g fiber

zucchini soup

MAKES 4 SERVINGS

If you have access to a bountiful harvest of zucchini, here's an enticing way to use it. Young zucchini are the most tender, but if you're inundated with ones the size of baseball bats, this soup provides an excellent solution for what to do with them.

¼ cup extra-virgin olive oil

3 cups diced red onions

6 cups diced zucchini

1 medium potato, peeled and diced

2 teaspoons herbes de Provence

½ teaspoon sea salt

3 cups unsweetened almond milk or Basic Almond Milk (page 9)

1 cup thinly sliced scallions

Freshly ground black pepper

1 tablespoon snipped fresh chives or additional sliced scallions, for garnish

Put the oil in a large soup pot over medium-high heat. When the oil is hot, add the onions and cook, stirring frequently, until soft and beginning to lightly brown, about 10 minutes. Add the zucchini and potato and stir well. Cook, stirring constantly, until the vegetables begin to stick, about 4 minutes. Add the herbes de Provence and salt and cook, stirring constantly, for 1 minute. Stir in the almond milk and bring to a boil. Decrease the heat to medium, cover, and cook, stirring occasionally, until the vegetables are tender, about 15 minutes.

Scoop out about 3 cups of the mixture and put it in a blender. Add the scallions and process on high speed until smooth. Pour into the pot and stir until well combined. Heat over medium heat, stirring frequently, until hot. Season with pepper to taste. Garnish with the chives and serve at once.

Per serving: 274 calories, 7 g protein, 17 g fat (2 g sat), 30 g carbohydrates, 433 mg sodium, 410 mg calcium, 6 g fiber

Note: Analysis doesn't include freshly ground black pepper to taste.

creamy black bean soup

Black beans, like chocolate, are a food of the gods. With their deep, rich flavor and dense creaminess, they meld flawlessly with almond milk in this silky-smooth soup.

1½ cups coarsely chopped **tomatoes**

½ **onion,** cut into chunks

4 cloves **garlic**

½ teaspoon **dried ground chiles** or crushed **red pepper flakes,** or 2 tablespoons dried ground ancho or pasilla chiles

½ teaspoon **sea salt**

1 tablespoon extra-virgin **olive oil**

1½ cups finely diced **onions**

2 cups no-salt-added **vegetable broth** or water

4 cups no-salt-added cooked or canned **black beans,** rinsed if canned

3 cups unsweetened **almond milk** or Basic Almond Milk (page 9)

½ cup coarsely chopped fresh **cilantro leaves**

3 tablespoons freshly squeezed **lime juice**

Freshly ground **black pepper**

Put the tomatoes, onion chunks, garlic, ground chiles, and salt in a blender and process on high speed until smooth.

Put the oil in a large soup pot over medium-high heat. When the oil is hot, add the diced onions and stir well. Spread the onions out to evenly coat the bottom of the pot. Decrease the heat to low, cover, and cook, stirring occasionally and spreading out the onions again, for 10 minutes. If the onions are sticking, add 1 tablespoon of water. Do not let the onions brown.

Increase the heat to high, add the tomato mixture, and stir until well combined. Cook, stirring frequently, until the mixture is very thick and nearly dry, about 15 minutes. Add the broth, stir well, and bring to a boil. Cook, stirring occasionally, until the liquid is reduced by about half, about 5 minutes.

Transfer the mixture to a blender, add 2 cups of the beans, and process on high speed until smooth. Pour into the pot. Add the remaining 2 cups of beans and the almond milk and heat over medium heat, stirring frequently, until hot. Stir in the cilantro and cook, stirring almost constantly, for 1 minute. Remove from the heat and stir in the lime juice. Season with pepper to taste. Serve at once.

Almonds are the most nutritionally dense nut, whether compared per calorie or per ounce.

Per serving: 418 calories, 22 g protein, 8 g fat (1 g sat), 68 g carbohydrates, 463 mg sodium, 501 mg calcium, 20 g fiber

Note: Analysis doesn't include freshly ground black pepper to taste.

roasted cauliflower soup WITH PEAS

MAKES 6 SERVINGS

Roasting cauliflower utterly transforms both its texture and flavor. In combination here with Indian spices and peas, this relatively mild vegetable becomes truly majestic.

    2 pounds **cauliflower**, cut or broken into bite-sized florets
    5 tablespoons extra-virgin **olive oil**
    ½ teaspoon **sea salt**
    3 cups finely diced **onions**
    1 large **potato**, peeled and diced
    7 cloves **garlic**, minced
    1 tablespoon **curry powder**
    2 cups no-salt-added **vegetable broth** or water
    2½ cups unsweetened **almond milk** or Basic Almond Milk
       (page 9)
    1 cup fresh or frozen **peas**
    ¼ cup coarsely chopped fresh **cilantro leaves**

Preheat the oven to 375 degrees F. Line a rimmed baking sheet with parchment paper.

Put the cauliflower in a large bowl. Add 3 tablespoons of the oil and the salt and toss until evenly distributed. Spread the cauliflower in a single layer on the lined baking sheet. Bake, stirring every 10 minutes to prevent burning, until evenly browned and tender, about 40 minutes.

Put the remaining 2 tablespoons of oil in a large soup pot over medium-high heat. When the oil is hot, add the onions and stir well. Spread the onions out to evenly cover the bottom of the pot. Decrease the heat to low, cover, and cook, stirring occasionally and spreading out the mixture again, for 15 minutes. If the onions are sticking, add 1 tablespoon of water. Do not let the onions brown.

Increase the heat to medium-high and add the potato and garlic. Cook, stirring constantly, for 3 minutes. Add the curry powder and cook, stirring constantly, for 1 minute. Add the broth and bring to a boil. Decrease the heat to medium and cook until the potato is tender and the liquid is reduced to about 1 cup, about 15 minutes. Add the cauliflower and stir well.

Scoop out about half the soup and put in a blender. Add the almond milk and process on high speed until smooth. Pour into the pot.

Bring 2 cups of water to a boil in a small saucepan. Add the peas and cook until just tender, about 5 minutes. Drain well and add to the soup.

Heat the soup over medium heat, stirring constantly to prevent sticking, until hot. Garnish with the cilantro and serve at once.

Per serving: 245 calories, 7 g protein, 13 g fat (1 g sat), 29 g carbohydrates, 341 mg sodium, 254 mg calcium, 7 g fiber

roasted parsnip soup

MAKES 4 SERVINGS

Parsnips are an underappreciated vegetable, possibly because they look a bit like mutant, anemic carrots. They are, however, quite delicious, and roasting brings out the best in them. This soup should win over even the most parsnip-averse diners.

 1 pound **parsnips,** peeled and cut into 1-inch chunks
 1 **onion,** quartered
 2 tablespoons **coconut oil,** melted
 ½ teaspoon **sea salt**
 2 cups no-salt-added **vegetable broth** or water
 3 cups unsweetened **almond milk** or Basic Almond Milk (page 9)
 1 tablespoon **maple syrup,** plus more as needed
 ½ teaspoon ground **allspice**
 ½ teaspoon ground **ginger**
 ½ teaspoon ground **mace**
 1 tablespoon freshly squeezed **lemon juice**
   Freshly ground **black pepper**

Preheat the oven to 350 degrees F. Line a rimmed baking sheet with parchment paper.

Put the parsnips, onion, oil, and salt in a large bowl. Toss until the vegetables are thoroughly coated with the oil and salt. Spread in a single layer on the lined baking sheet and bake for 45 minutes, stirring every 15 minutes to prevent burning, until the vegetables are tender and browned.

Transfer the vegetables to a large soup pot, add the broth, and bring to a boil over medium-high heat. Decrease the heat to medium and cook, stirring occasionally, until the vegetables are very soft and almost all the liquid is absorbed, about 20 minutes. Transfer to a blender. Add the almond milk and process on high speed until smooth. Pour into the pot and whisk in the maple syrup, allspice, ginger, and mace. Heat over medium heat, stirring frequently, until hot. Remove from the heat and stir in the lemon juice. Season with pepper to taste and additional maple syrup if desired. Serve at once.

Per serving: 188 calories, 3 g protein, 10 g fat (6 g sat), 23 g carbohydrates, 417 mg sodium, 351 mg calcium, 7 g fiber
Note: Analysis doesn't include freshly ground black pepper to taste.

Grazing the Salad Bowl

C H A P T E R

6

romaine salad WITH PUMPKIN SEED DRESSING

MAKES 4 SERVINGS

Toasted pumpkin seeds join almond milk and a little lemon juice and garlic to make a luxuriously creamy dressing that elevates this crisp romaine salad to extravagant heights.

- ¾ cup **raw pumpkin seeds**
- 1¼ cups unsweetened **almond milk** or Basic Almond Milk (page 9)
- 6 tablespoons freshly squeezed **lemon juice**
- 2 small cloves **garlic**
- ¼ teaspoon **sea salt**
- 12 cups bite-sized cut or torn **romaine lettuce**
- 1 medium **English cucumber**, sliced
- 1 **green bell pepper**, cut into bite-sized pieces

To make the dressing, put the pumpkin seeds in a medium skillet over medium-high heat and toast, stirring frequently, until lightly browned and fragrant, about 5 minutes. Transfer the seeds to a small bowl and pour the almond milk over them. Let the seeds soak in the almond milk for 1 hour. Transfer the seeds and almond milk to a blender. Add the lemon juice, garlic, and salt and process on high speed until smooth (some small bits of pumpkin seeds will remain).

To make the salad, put the lettuce, cucumber, and bell pepper in a large bowl and toss well. Add the dressing and toss again. Serve at once.

Per serving: 176 calories, 8 g protein, 12 g fat (2 g sat), 14 g carbohydrates, 209 mg sodium, 206 mg calcium, 5 g fiber

arugula and tomato salad
WITH CREAMY BASIL DRESSING

MAKES 4 SERVINGS

Tomatoes and basil are an incredible flavor combination. In this recipe, they're brought together with almond milk to make a spectacular, creamy dressing. Brazil nuts add great texture to the dish, with a mouthfeel reminiscent of Parmesan cheese.

1	cup unsweetened **almond milk** or Basic Almond Milk (page 9)
¾	cup **Brazil nuts**, soaked in hot water 1 hour and drained
¼	cup fresh **basil leaves**, firmly packed
1½	tablespoons **sherry vinegar** or **white balsamic vinegar**
1	clove **garlic**
¼	teaspoon **sea salt**
⅛	teaspoon freshly ground **black pepper**
8	ounces **baby arugula**
4	small ripe **tomatoes**, quartered or cut into bite-sized pieces
1	small **red onion**, quartered and thinly sliced

To make the dressing, put the almond milk, Brazil nuts, basil, vinegar, garlic, salt, and pepper in a blender and process on high speed until smooth.

To make the salad, put the arugula, tomatoes, and onion in a large bowl and toss until well combined. Add the dressing and toss again. Serve at once.

Per serving: 229 calories, 7 g protein, 18 g fat (5 g sat), 13 g carbohydrates, 205 mg sodium, 258 mg calcium, 4 g fiber

argentine-style hearts of palm salad

MAKES 4 SERVINGS

Almond cream is an excellent replacement for the whipped cream that's traditionally used in this salad dressing because the distinctive flavors of the salad come from the other ingredients. This dressing is the best I've come across for showcasing hearts of palm.

1	**red bell pepper**
1	**green bell pepper**
1	head **frisée lettuce**
¾	cup **Almond Cream** (page 11)
6	tablespoons **ketchup**
3	tablespoons freshly squeezed **lime juice**
1	teaspoon **Tabasco sauce** or **sriracha sauce**
¼	teaspoon **sea salt**
⅛	teaspoon freshly ground **black pepper**
2½	cups sliced canned **hearts of palm** (½-inch slices)
2	ripe **avocados**, cut into 1-inch pieces
2	small ripe **tomatoes**, quartered or cut into bite-sized pieces
8	**scallions**, thinly sliced
2	tablespoons chopped fresh **parsley**

Preheat the broiler. Line a baking sheet with foil.

Quarter the red and green bell peppers lengthwise and arrange them skin-side up on the lined baking sheet. Broil until evenly blackened, about 7 minutes. Immediately put the bell peppers in a medium bowl, cover tightly, and let steam for 10 minutes. Pour cold water into the bowl to loosen the skins. Remove and discard the skins. Cut the roasted peppers into ¾-inch pieces.

Cut the root end off the lettuce and break up the individual frilly stems. Wash and spin dry or wrap in a clean tea towel and refrigerate until serving time.

Put the almond cream, ketchup, lime juice, Tabasco sauce, salt, and pepper in a large bowl. Whisk until thoroughly blended to a pink cream. Add the bell peppers, hearts of palm, avocados, tomatoes, and scallions and toss gently but thoroughly.

Divide the lettuce among four chilled plates, forming wide beds. Divide the hearts of palm mixture among the plates, forming attractive mounds in the center of the lettuce. Garnish generously with the parsley and serve at once.

Whole natural almonds will keep well for up to two years in the refrigerator. Their long storage life is due in part to their high vitamin E content, which helps keep them fresh.

Per serving: 374 calories, 11 g protein, 27 g fat (2 g sat), 29 g carbohydrates, 764 mg sodium, 191 mg calcium, 12 g fiber

Note: Analysis for the Almond Cream in this recipe is based on the almonds prior to straining.

potato salad with panache

MAKES 6 SERVINGS

This isn't the same old boring potato salad you're used to. Made with silky Yukon gold potatoes and a vibrantly flavored, rosy dressing, this is pumped-up potato salad designed for a new era.

3½ pounds Yukon **gold potatoes**, steamed or boiled until tender

2 cups **Tomato-Pepper Dressing** (opposite page)

12 **scallions**, thinly sliced

Juice of 1 **lemon**

Let the potatoes cool until they can be easily handled, then peel and dice them. Put the potatoes in a large bowl. Add the dressing, scallions, and lemon juice and gently stir until the potatoes are evenly coated and the scallions are evenly distributed. Serve at once or transfer to a storage container, seal tightly, and refrigerate for up to 4 days.

Per serving: 266 calories, 1 g protein, 5 g fat (1 g sat), 49 g carbohydrates, 359 mg sodium, 157 mg calcium, 7 g fiber

tomato-pepper dressing

MAKES 2 CUPS

This makes a lively, unusual, and healthy dressing. Serve it warm or cold on salads, pasta, steamed veggies, or even potato salad (see opposite page).

- 2 tablespoons extra-virgin olive oil
- 1 small onion, diced
- 1 teaspoon minced garlic
- 3 roasted red peppers, diced (see tip, page 13)
- ¼ cup no-salt-added tomato paste
- 1½ teaspoons sweet or hot smoked paprika or Hungarian hot paprika
- ½ teaspoon sea salt
- ⅛ teaspoon freshly ground black pepper
- 1½ cups unsweetened almond milk, Rich Almond Milk (page 10), or Basic Almond Milk (page 9)
- ¾ teaspoon arrowroot starch

Put the oil in a medium saucepan over medium-high heat. When the oil is hot, add the onion and cook, stirring frequently, until soft, about 5 minutes. Add the garlic and cook, stirring constantly, for 2 minutes. Add the bell peppers and stir to combine. Decrease the heat to medium and cook, stirring occasionally, for 4 minutes. Add the tomato paste, paprika, salt, and pepper and stir to combine.

Put the almond milk in a small bowl and whisk in the arrowroot. Add to the pepper mixture and stir until well combined. Bring to a simmer over medium-high heat, stirring almost constantly. Decrease the heat to medium-low and cook, stirring frequently, until the vegetables are very tender, about 20 minutes. Transfer to a blender and process on high speed until smooth. Use at once or let cool before using. Alternatively, transfer to a jar, seal tightly, and store in the refrigerator for up to 4 days.

Per ⅓ cup: 58 calories, 1 g protein, 5 g fat (1 g sat), 2 g carbohydrates, 275 mg sodium, 125 mg calcium, 1 g fiber

ranch dressing

MAKES 2½ CUPS

Ranch dressing has near-universal appeal. Creamy and tangy, with hints of herbs and buttermilk, it hits several pleasure points in the American palate.

- 1 cup **raw cashews,** soaked in hot water 1 hour and drained
- ¾ cup unsweetened **almond milk,** Rich Almond Milk (page 10), **or Basic Almond Milk** (page 9)
- ¾ cup unsweetened plain coconut **yogurt** or soy yogurt
- 3 tablespoons freshly squeezed **lemon juice** or **white wine vinegar**
- 1 teaspoon minced **garlic**
- ½ teaspoon **sea salt**
- ⅛ teaspoon freshly ground **black pepper**
- 6 tablespoons chopped fresh **chives** or **scallions**
- 2 tablespoons chopped fresh **parsley**

Put the cashews, almond milk, yogurt, lemon juice, garlic, salt, and pepper in a blender and process on high speed until smooth. Add the chives and parsley and pulse until the mixture turns pale green and is flecked with bits of the herbs. Use at once or transfer to a jar, seal tightly, and store in the refrigerator for up to 4 days.

Per 2 tablespoons: 40 calories, 1 g protein, 3 g fat (1 g sat), 3 g carbohydrates, 63 mg sodium, 23 mg calcium, 1 g fiber

pine nut dressing

MAKES 1¼ CUPS

Roasting improves the flavor of all nuts, but pine nuts in particular are transformed by this process. This creamy dressing is marvelous on any crisp green salad. It's so good, you might just want to serve it on lettuce alone, with no other ingredients to detract from its sublime taste.

- 2 tablespoons extra-virgin **olive oil**
- 2 cloves **garlic**, cut in half lengthwise
- ¾ cup **pine nuts**
- ½ cup unsweetened **almond milk**, Rich Almond Milk (page 10), **or Basic Almond Milk** (page 9)
- 2 tablespoons freshly squeezed **lemon juice**
- 1 teaspoon **mellow white miso**
- ⅛ teaspoon **sea salt**

Put the oil in a small saucepan over medium heat. When the oil is hot, add the garlic and cook, stirring constantly, until the garlic turns light tan, 2 to 3 minutes. Remove the garlic with a slotted spoon and transfer to a blender. Add the pine nuts to the saucepan and cook, stirring or swirling the pan constantly, until they turn light brown. Reserve ¼ cup of the pine nuts and add the rest of the nuts along with the oil to the blender. Add the almond milk, lemon juice, miso, and salt to the blender and process on high speed until smooth. Add the reserved pine nuts and pulse briefly, just until coarsely chopped. Use at once or transfer to a jar, seal tightly, and store in the refrigerator for up to 4 days.

Per 2 tablespoons: 97 calories, 1 g protein, 10 g fat (1 g sat), 2 g carbohydrates, 58 mg sodium, 26 mg calcium, 1 g fiber

Mains and Sides

spiral pasta WITH ROASTED PEPPER SAUCE

MAKES 4 SERVINGS

This bright-red cream sauce is laden with layers of flavor so delicious you could eat it with a spoon. It's paired here with spiral pasta, which captures just the right amount of sauce to transport it directly to your eagerly waiting taste buds.

2 tablespoons extra-virgin **olive oil**

1 cup diced **onion**

3 cups diced **roasted red peppers** (see tip, page 13)

2 cloves **garlic**, minced

½ teaspoon **sea salt**

½ teaspoon **hot smoked paprika**

¼ teaspoon **cayenne**

1 cup **water**

1 **bay leaf**

2 cups unsweetened **almond milk** or Basic Almond Milk (page 9)

1 pound **spiral pasta**, such as fusilli, rotelle, or gemelli

1 tablespoon chopped fresh **parsley**, for garnish

Put the oil in a large saucepan over medium-high heat. When the oil is hot, add the onion and cook, stirring frequently, until soft, about 5 minutes. Add the red peppers and garlic, and cook, stirring constantly, until nearly dry, about 3 minutes. Add the salt, paprika, and cayenne and stir well. Add the water and bay leaf.

Decrease the heat to medium-low and cook, stirring occasionally, until the vegetables are tender and nearly dry, about 15 minutes. Add the almond milk and stir until well combined. Increase the heat to medium-high and cook, stirring frequently, until the almond milk is reduced by about half, about 5 minutes. Remove and discard the bay leaf. Transfer to a blender and process on high speed until smooth. Return to the saucepan, cover, and keep warm.

Cook the pasta in boiling water according to the package directions. Drain and add to the sauce. Toss well. Garnish with the parsley and serve at once.

Per serving: 490 calories, 15 g protein, 10 g fat (1 g sat), 90 g carbohydrates, 700 mg sodium, 414 mg calcium, 1 g fiber

gemelli WITH ZUCCHINI, BASIL, AND CREAM

MAKES 4 SERVINGS

Gemelli derives from the Italian word for "twins." The pasta looks like two tubes wound around each other but in fact is made from just a single strand doubled over and twisted into a spiral.

    3 tablespoons extra-virgin **olive oil**
    2 medium **onions,** cut lengthwise into strips
    8 small **zucchini,** cut into thin, 2-inch-long sticks
       (about 6 cups)
    2 cloves **garlic,** minced
    ½ teaspoon **sea salt**
    ⅛ teaspoon freshly ground **black pepper**
    2 cups unsweetened **almond milk,** Rich Almond Milk
       (page 10), **or Basic Almond Milk** (page 9)
    ½ cup fresh **basil leaves,** firmly packed
    1 pound **gemelli** or fusilli

Put the oil in a large saucepan over medium-high heat. When the oil is hot, add the onions and cook, stirring frequently, until soft, about 5 minutes. Add the zucchini, garlic, and salt. Cook, stirring frequently, until the zucchini begins to soften, about 5 minutes. Decrease the heat to medium-low and cook, stirring frequently, until the zucchini is tender but firm, about 5 minutes. Add the pepper and stir to combine. Stir in the almond milk. Increase the heat to high and cook, stirring occasionally, until the almond milk is reduced by about half, about 5 minutes. Chop the basil coarsely and stir it into the mixture. Remove from the heat, cover, and keep warm.

Cook the pasta in boiling water according to the package directions. Drain and add to the sauce. Toss well and serve at once.

Per serving: 573 calories, 21 g protein, 14 g fat (6 g sat), 98 g carbohydrates, 407 mg sodium, 293 mg calcium, 5 g fiber

linguine WITH OLIVE SAUCE

This recipe is so simple, you don't even need to add salt, because the olives add more than enough. Just have some crusty bread handy for mopping up the sauce in the bottom of the bowl after the pasta is gone. You're going to love this dish!

> 2 cups unsweetened **almond milk,** Rich Almond Milk (page 10), **or Basic Almond Milk** (page 9)
>
> 1½ teaspoons **arrowroot starch**
>
> ¾ cup pitted **kalamata olives,** rinsed
>
> Freshly ground **black pepper**
>
> 1 pound **linguine**

Put the almond milk in a small saucepan and whisk in the arrowroot starch. Bring to a boil over medium-high heat, whisking occasionally. Decrease the heat to medium and cook, whisking frequently, until thickened and reduced to about 1½ cups, about 5 minutes.

Put the olives in a blender and pour the thickened almond milk over them. Process on high speed until smooth (some small bits of olives may remain). Pour into the saucepan and season with pepper to taste. Heat over medium heat, stirring occasionally, until hot. Remove from the heat and cover to keep warm.

Cook the pasta in boiling water according to the package directions. Drain, reserving ½ cup of the cooking liquid, and return to the pot. Add the sauce, using a silicone spatula to scrape every last bit into the pot, and toss well. If the sauce thickens too much, add a little of the reserved cooking liquid and toss again. Serve at once.

Per serving: 460 calories, 15 g protein, 5 g fat (1 g sat), 85 g carbohydrates, 355 mg sodium, 225 mg calcium, 5 g fiber
Note: Analysis doesn't include freshly ground black pepper to taste.

bow ties WITH CREAMY TOMATO SAUCE

MAKES 4 SERVINGS

Bow-tie pasta, also called *farfalle,* which means "butterflies" in Italian, has a fun shape that's particularly well suited for catching and transporting a generous amount of this beguiling sauce to your mouth.

2 tablespoons extra-virgin **olive oil**

½ small **onion,** minced

½ stalk **celery,** minced

½ **carrot,** minced

2 cloves **garlic,** minced

2 cups no-salt-added **tomato purée**

½ teaspoon **sea salt,** plus more as needed

1½ cups unsweetened **almond milk,** Rich Almond Milk (page 10), **or** Basic Almond Milk (page 9)

1 teaspoon **arrowroot starch**

½ cup fresh **basil leaves,** firmly packed

Freshly ground **black pepper**

12 ounces **bow-tie pasta**

Put the oil in a medium saucepan over medium-high heat. When the oil is hot, add the onion, celery, carrot, and garlic and stir to combine. When the vegetables begin to sizzle, decrease the heat to low, cover, and cook, stirring occasionally, until the vegetables are very tender, about 20 minutes. Stir in the tomato purée and the salt and increase the heat to medium. Cook, stirring frequently, for 10 minutes. Remove from the heat and cover to keep warm.

While the tomato mixture is cooking, put the almond milk in a medium saucepan and whisk in the arrowroot. Bring to a boil over medium-high heat, whisking occasionally. Decrease the heat to medium and cook, whisking occasionally, until thickened and reduced to about 1 cup, about 5 minutes. Add to the tomato mixture and stir well to combine. Warm over low heat. Tear the basil into bite-sized pieces and stir into the sauce. Season with pepper and additional salt to taste if desired. Cover to keep warm.

Cook the pasta in boiling water according to the package directions. Drain, reserving ½ cup of the cooking liquid, and return to the pot. Add the sauce and toss well. If the mixture is too thick, add a little of the reserved cooking liquid and toss again. Serve at once.

Per serving: 543 calories, 17 g protein, 10 g fat (1 g sat), 97 g carbohydrates, 119 mg sodium, 198 mg calcium, 6 g fiber

orecchiete WITH BASIL CREAM SAUCE

MAKES 4 SERVINGS

Orecchiete is Italian for "little ears." The shape is ideal for creamy sauces, as it holds a generous amount in its curved crevices. If you can't find this pasta, small shells (*conchiglie*) would make a fine alternative.

2 cups unsweetened **almond milk,** Rich Almond Milk (page 10), **or Basic Almond Milk** (page 9)

1½ teaspoons **arrowroot starch**

1 tablespoon extra-virgin **olive oil**

1 small clove **garlic,** cut in half lengthwise

2 tablespoons **pine nuts** (optional)

1 cup fresh **basil leaves,** firmly packed

Sea salt

Freshly ground **black pepper**

1 pound **orecchiete** or small shell pasta

Put the almond milk in a small bowl and whisk in the arrowroot starch.

Put the olive oil and garlic in a medium saucepan over medium-high heat. Tip the pan to form a small pool of the oil at the side and cook until the garlic just begins to brown, about 2 minutes. Transfer the garlic to a blender.

Add the optional pine nuts to the oil remaining in the saucepan and cook, stirring constantly, until the nuts are lightly golden. Whisk the almond milk mixture again and pour into the pan. Cook, whisking frequently, until thickened and reduced to about 1½ cups, about 5 minutes.

Put the basil in the blender and pour the hot almond milk mixture over it. Process on high speed until smooth. Pour into the saucepan and season with salt and pepper to taste. Cover to keep warm.

Cook the pasta in boiling water according to the package directions. Drain, reserving ½ cup of the cooking liquid, and return to the pot. Add the sauce, using a silicone spatula to scrape every last bit into the pot, and toss well. If the sauce thickens too much, add a little of the reserved cooking liquid and toss again. Serve at once.

Per serving: 462 calories, 1 g protein, 5 g fat (1 g sat), 2 g carbohydrates, 81 mg sodium, 244 mg calcium, 1 g fiber

Note: Analysis doesn't include sea salt or freshly ground black pepper to taste.

fettuccine WITH PORTOBELLO CREAM SAUCE

MAKES 4 SERVINGS

Properly handled, almond milk can closely mimic the character of cream, which is very important in a dish like this where the flavors are built up in subtle layers and then bound into a thickened sauce. Fettuccine is the ideal noodle for this dish, as it collects just the right amount of sauce on the individual ribbons as they twirl around the fork.

4 large portobello **mushrooms**

3 tablespoons extra-virgin **olive oil**

½ cup finely diced **onion**

¼ teaspoon **sea salt**

1 cup no-salt-added **vegetable broth** or water

1 sprig fresh **rosemary**

1 sprig fresh **thyme**

1 **bay leaf**

1½ cups unsweetened **almond milk,** Rich Almond Milk (page 10), **or** Basic Almond Milk (page 9)

¾ teaspoon **arrowroot starch**

Freshly ground **black pepper**

1 pound **fettuccine**

1 tablespoon freshly squeezed **lemon juice**

1 tablespoon chopped fresh **parsley,** for garnish

Wash the mushroom caps and pat them dry. Gently work the stems free and discard. Carefully scrape the dark gills out from the underside of the caps with a small spoon. Dice the mushrooms by slicing each cap horizontally and then slicing it crosswise.

Put the oil in a large saucepan over medium-high heat. When the oil is hot, add the onion and cook, stirring frequently, until soft, about 5 minutes. Continue cooking, stirring constantly, until the onion begins to brown, about 2 minutes. Add the mushrooms and stir well. Cook, stirring frequently, until the mushrooms have released their liquid, about 2 minutes. Continue cooking, stirring frequently, until the liquid is absorbed and the mushrooms are beginning to brown, about 3 minutes longer. Add the salt and stir well. Add the broth, rosemary, thyme, and bay leaf. Decrease the heat to medium-low and cook, stirring occasionally, until the vegetables are tender and nearly dry, about 15 minutes.

Put the almond milk and arrowroot starch in a small bowl or measuring cup and whisk to combine. Pour into the saucepan, stirring well. Increase the heat to high and cook, stirring frequently, until the almond milk has thickened and slightly reduced, about 4 minutes. Season with pepper to taste. Remove from the heat, cover, and keep warm.

Cook the pasta in boiling water according to the package directions. Drain, reserving ½ cup of the cooking liquid, and return to the pot. Reheat the mushroom sauce if necessary. Remove and discard the rosemary and thyme sprigs and the bay leaf. Stir in the lemon juice and season with pepper to taste. Add the sauce to the pasta and toss well. If the sauce thickens too much, add a little of the reserved cooking liquid and toss again. Garnish with the parsley and serve at once.

Per serving: 539 calories, 17 g protein, 14 g fat (2 g sat), 90 g carbohydrates, 214 mg sodium, 185 mg calcium, 6 g fiber

Note: Analysis doesn't include freshly ground black pepper to taste.

mac 'n' cheese

MAKES 6 SERVINGS

There are many versions of macaroni and cheese. This one is an adaptation of the original great-granddaddy of them all, *pasta al gratine*. It's irresistible.

- 6 tablespoons **vegan butter**
- 12 ounces **vegan cheese**, grated
- 12 ounces **macaroni**
- ¼ cup unbleached all-purpose **white flour**
- 2 cups unsweetened **almond milk** or Rich Almond Milk (page 10)
- 6 tablespoons **nutritional yeast flakes**
- 1 teaspoon **sea salt**
- ¼ teaspoon freshly ground **black pepper**
- Pinch **cayenne**

Preheat the oven to 425 degrees F. Grease a 2-quart casserole dish with 2 tablespoons of the butter and sprinkle in the cheese. Shake the dish to coat the bottom and sides with the cheese. Pour out the excess cheese and set it aside.

Cook the macaroni in boiling water according to the package directions. Drain in a colander and rinse under cold running water. Drain well and transfer to a large bowl.

Put the remaining 4 tablespoons of butter in a medium saucepan over medium heat. When the butter is melted, whisk in the flour and cook, whisking frequently, until the mixture turns light brown, about 2 minutes. Gradually add the almond milk in a stream, whisking vigorously. When the mixture thickens, add the nutritional yeast, salt, and pepper and whisk to combine. Remove from the heat and stir in half the remaining cheese. Scrape the mixture into the bowl with the macaroni and stir until well combined. Spoon into the prepared baking dish and smooth the top. Sprinkle with the remaining cheese.

Bake for about 20 minutes, until bubbling and browned on top. Serve at once.

Per serving: 642 calories, 12 g protein, 37 g fat (7 g sat), 63 g carbohydrates, 1,028 mg sodium, 150 mg calcium, 4 g fiber

mushrooms in almond cream

MAKES 4 SERVINGS

Any kind of mushroom can be used in this dish, although wild mushrooms are especially recommended for their heady, woodsy perfume. A splash of lemon juice at the end is ideal for bringing out the flavor of the mushrooms and adding a spark of freshness to the dish.

2 tablespoons extra-virgin **olive oil**

3 tablespoons finely diced **shallots** or onion

1 pound button or cremini **mushrooms**, quartered lengthwise

¼ teaspoon **sea salt**, plus more as needed

1 cup unsweetened **almond milk**, Rich Almond Milk (page 10), or Basic Almond Milk (page 9)

½ teaspoon **arrowroot starch**

1 tablespoon chopped fresh **parsley**

1 tablespoon freshly squeezed **lemon juice**

Freshly ground **black pepper**

Put the oil a large skillet over medium heat. When the oil is hot, add the shallots and cook, stirring frequently, until soft and translucent, about 7 minutes. Increase the heat to medium-high and add the mushrooms. Cover and cook until the mushrooms begin to release their juices, about 1 minute. Uncover and stir in the salt. Increase the heat to high and cook, stirring frequently, until the mushrooms are nearly dry, about 5 minutes. Put the almond milk in a measuring cup or small bowl and whisk in the arrowroot starch until well incorporated. Pour into the skillet and stir well. Decrease the heat to medium and cook, stirring frequently, until the milk thickens and the mushrooms are evenly coated, about 5 minutes. Stir in the parsley and lemon juice. Season with pepper to taste. Serve at once.

Per serving: 98 calories, 4 g protein, 8 g fat (1 g sat), 5 g carbohydrates, 187 mg sodium, 115 mg calcium, 1 g fiber

Note: Analysis doesn't include freshly ground black pepper to taste.

vegetable pot pie

MAKES 6 SERVINGS

Few things are better comfort food than a hot, bubbling pot pie. The creamy, luscious interior contrasts beautifully with the flaky, buttery crust. The mix of tender vegetables in this irresistible rendition raises the bar, transforming this simple dish into a complete meal.

14 tablespoons **vegan butter**

2 cups diced **onions**

¾ cup diced **celery**

1½ cups diced **carrots**

1½ cups diced **rutabaga** (peel before dicing if waxed)

1½ cups fresh or frozen cut **green beans**

1½ cups fresh or frozen **peas**

1½ cups no-salt-added **vegetable broth**

¼ cup chopped fresh **parsley**

1¾ cups unbleached all-purpose **white flour**

1½ cups unsweetened **almond milk** or Rich Almond Milk (page 10)

1½ teaspoons **sea salt**

⅛ teaspoon freshly grated **nutmeg** or ground nutmeg

Freshly ground **black pepper**

1 tablespoon freshly squeezed **lemon juice**

3 tablespoons **ice water,** plus more as needed

Put 2 tablespoons of the butter in a large saucepan over medium-high heat. When the butter is melted, add the onions and celery and cook, stirring frequently, until the vegetables are soft, about 10 minutes. Add the carrots, rutabaga, green beans, peas, broth, and parsley and bring to a boil. Decrease the heat to medium and cook, stirring frequently, until the vegetables are tender and the broth is nearly absorbed, about 7 minutes.

Preheat the oven to 400 degrees F.

Grease a 13 x 9-inch baking dish with 1 tablespoon of the butter.

Put 4 tablespoons of the butter in a small saucepan over medium-high heat. When the butter is melted, whisk in ½ cup of the flour and cook, whisking constantly, until the mixture begins to color slightly, about 2 minutes. Whisk in the almond milk and cook, whisking constantly, until the mixture thickens, about 1 minute. Stir in ¾ teaspoon of the salt and the nutmeg and season with pepper to taste. Add the mixture to the vegetables and stir until well combined. Stir in the lemon juice. Pour the vegetable mixture into the prepared baking dish, spreading it out evenly.

Put the remaining 1¼ cups flour and remaining ¾ teaspoon salt in a medium bowl and stir to combine. Cut the remaining 7 tablespoons of butter into 1-tablespoon pieces and add to the flour mixture. Pinch the butter into the flour with your fingertips, mixing until about half the butter is blended into the flour and the rest is in pieces about 1 teaspoon in size. Add the ice water and stir with a fork until the dough comes together. If the mixture is too dry, add a little more water, 1 teaspoon at a time, until a dough forms. Several unblended pieces of the butter will remain. Roll the dough out on a lightly floured board into a 14 x 10-inch rectangle. Transfer to the top of the baking dish and press down lightly over the filling. Roll the edges over and crimp.

Bake the pot pie for about 40 minutes, until the crust is golden brown and the filling is bubbling. Serve at once.

Per serving: 466 calories, 7 g protein, 27 g fat (7 g sat), 46 g carbohydrates, 1,045 mg sodium, 165 mg calcium, 6 g fiber

Note: Analysis doesn't include freshly ground black pepper to taste.

tofu WITH TOASTED SESAME SAUCE

MAKES 6 SERVINGS

Tofu is bland, like a blank canvas onto which any wild creation can be applied. This dish is all about the lip-smacking sauce, and the tofu is merely the vehicle that accentuates and carries it straight to your anticipating mouth.

2 pounds **extra-firm tofu**, gently squeezed or pressed, or super-firm tofu

6 tablespoons reduced-sodium **tamari**

1 cup **raw sesame seeds**

2 cups unsweetened **almond milk** or Basic Almond Milk (page 9)

¼ cup **mellow white miso**

Zest of 2 **lemons** (remove the zest before juicing the lemons)

2 tablespoons freshly squeezed **lemon juice**

2 tablespoons **coconut oil**

2 **scallions**, thinly sliced

Preheat the oven to 200 degrees F.

Cut each block of tofu lengthwise into 6 equal slices (12 slices in all) and arrange them in a single layer on two large plates. Pour 4 tablespoons of the tamari over the tofu (2 tablespoons per plate), tipping the plates to spread it around as evenly as possible. Let marinate for 10 to 15 minutes before proceeding.

Put the sesame seeds in a small skillet over medium-high heat and toast, stirring constantly, until lightly browned and fragrant, about 5 minutes. Transfer to a blender and add the almond milk, miso, the remaining 2 tablespoons of tamari, and the lemon zest and juice. Process on high speed until smooth.

Put 1 tablespoon of the oil in a large skillet over medium-high heat. When the oil is melted, put 6 slices of the tofu in a single layer in the skillet. Brown the tofu lightly on each side, about 4 minutes per side. Carefully transfer to a baking sheet and put in the oven to keep warm. Repeat with the remaining oil and tofu.

To serve, put the tofu on individual plates or a large platter. Drizzle the sauce over the tofu, letting it pool. Garnish with the scallions and serve at once.

TIP If you have a high-speed blender, the blending process will warm the sauce. If you don't have a high-speed blender, transfer the sauce to a small saucepan and warm over low heat before serving.

ALMOND MILK ISN'T FOR INFANTS

Almond milk doesn't contain the vital nutrients in breast milk and baby formula, so it isn't an acceptable substitute for feeding infants. In addition, feeding almond milk to infants may cause them to develop a sensitivity to tree nuts. Speak to your doctor before giving almond milk to your infant.

Per serving: 449 calories, 31 g protein, 31 g fat (9 g sat), 13 g carbohydrates, 909 mg sodium, 588 mg calcium, 4 g fiber

zucchini pappardelle WITH CORN CREAM

MAKES 4 SERVINGS

Pappardelle are flat noodles about one inch wide that are usually served with rich creamy sauces and gravies. In this dish, thinly sliced zucchini stand in for the pasta. Look for young zucchini, not much thicker than your thumb, for the best results.

2 tablespoons extra-virgin **olive oil**

1 cup finely diced **white onion**

2 cups fresh or frozen **corn kernels**

1 cup unsweetened **almond milk** or Basic Almond Milk (page 9)

1 clove **garlic**, minced

¼ teaspoon **sea salt**, plus more as needed

3 tablespoons snipped fresh **chives**

2 pounds **zucchini**, thinly sliced lengthwise (see tip)

Freshly ground **black pepper**

Put the oil and onion in a large saucepan over medium heat and stir well. Spread the onion out to evenly cover the bottom of the saucepan. Decrease the heat to low, cover, and cook, stirring occasionally and spreading out the onion again, for 30 minutes. If the onion is sticking, add 1 tablespoon of water. Do not let the onion brown.

The flavonoids in almond skins work in synergy with the vitamin E in the nut, helping to reduce the risk of heart disease.

Add the corn, almond milk, garlic, and salt, and stir to combine. Increase the heat to medium-high and bring to a boil, stirring constantly. Decrease the heat to medium and cook, stirring frequently, until the corn is tender, about 8 minutes. Transfer to a blender and process on high speed until smooth. Return to the saucepan and cook over medium heat, stirring occasionally, until the sauce is thick enough to coat a spoon, about 10 minutes. Add 2 tablespoons of the chives and stir to combine.

Fill a large saucepan halfway with water and bring to a boil over high heat. Add the zucchini and cook, stirring occasionally, until just tender, 1 to 2 minutes. Drain well and add to the sauce. Toss gently but thoroughly. Season with salt and pepper to taste and toss again. Garnish with the remaining tablespoon of chives and serve at once.

 A mandoline is very helpful for obtaining thin, uniform slices of zucchini.

Per serving: 196 calories, 5 g protein, 8 g fat (1 g sat), 27 g carbohydrates, 205 mg sodium, 210 mg calcium, 5 g fiber

Note: Analysis doesn't include sea salt or freshly ground black pepper to taste.

cauliflower-stuffed potatoes

MAKES 2 SERVINGS

Twice-baked potatoes are a comfort food in a class of their own. This spiced-up version is a world apart from the usual stuffed spud, but it still retains the full comfort factor.

    4 medium **russet potatoes** (about 2½ pounds), scrubbed
    2 tablespoons **coconut oil**
    1 cup diced **onion**
    ½ teaspoon **sea salt**
    1 **tomato**, grated
    1 tablespoon **curry powder**
    1 small head **cauliflower**, cut or broken into small florets
    ½ cup **water**
    ¾ cup unsweetened **almond milk** or Basic Almond Milk (page 9)
    ½ cup chopped fresh **cilantro** or **parsley**

Preheat the oven to 400 degrees F.

Pierce the potatoes in several places with a fork to release steam as they bake and put them directly on oven rack at least two inches apart. Bake for 1 to 1½ hours, until the flesh can be easily pierced with a fork. When the potatoes are cool enough to handle, cut them in half lengthwise and carefully scoop out the flesh, leaving a thin layer in the skins to help them hold their shape. Chop the flesh coarsely.

Eating a daily handful of almonds a day may lower LDL, or "bad," cholesterol.

Put the oil in a large saucepan over medium-high heat. When the oil is melted, add the onion and salt and stir well. Decrease the heat to medium and cook, stirring frequently, until the onion is soft, about 5 minutes. Add the tomato and curry powder and stir well. Cover and cook, stirring occasionally, for 15 minutes. Increase the heat to medium-high and add the cauliflower. Cook, stirring constantly, until the mixture begins to dry out, about 2 minutes. Add the water and stir to combine. Decrease the heat to medium-low, cover, and cook, stirring frequently, until the cauliflower is tender, about 15 minutes. If the mixture is sticking, add 2 to 3 tablespoons of water during cooking as needed.

When the cauliflower is tender, add the potato flesh and stir to combine. Stir in the almond milk and increase the heat to medium-high. Cook, stirring and mashing the mixture slightly to create a soft but chunky texture, until hot. Remove from the heat and stir in the cilantro.

Fill the potato skins with the cauliflower mixture, mounding it slightly. Arrange the filled potatoes in a baking dish large enough to hold them all and bake for about 15 minutes, or until sizzling hot. Serve at once.

Per serving: 426 calories, 12 g protein, 15 g fat (12 g sat), 64 g carbohydrates, 665 mg sodium, 223 mg calcium, 11 g fiber

creamed greens

MAKES 4 SERVINGS

Like most creamy dishes, this is a comfort food. It can be made with green, red, or rainbow Swiss chard, spinach, or a combination of chard and spinach. Baby kale and other tender young greens could also be used, but mature greens would need to be cooked in advance as they won't have sufficient time in the pan to become tender.

8 cups stemmed and coarsely chopped **Swiss chard** or **spinach**, packed

2 tablespoons extra-virgin **olive oil**

1½ cups diced **onions**

¼ teaspoon **sea salt,** plus more as needed

2 cups unsweetened **almond milk,** Rich Almond Milk (page 10), or Basic Almond Milk (page 9)

1 teaspoon **arrowroot starch**

⅛ teaspoon freshly grated **nutmeg** or ground nutmeg (optional)

Freshly ground **black pepper**

Bring a large pot of water to a boil over high heat and add the Swiss chard. Cook for about 1 minute, or until the chard is as tender as you like. Drain in a colander. Shake the colander and press the chard to express as much water as possible. Chop the chard coarsely.

Put the oil in a large saucepan over medium heat. When the oil is hot, stir in the onions, decrease the heat to low, cover, and cook, stirring occasionally, until the onions are very soft, about 10 minutes. Uncover and increase the heat to medium-high. Stir in the salt and cook, stirring constantly, for 1 minute.

Put the almond milk in a measuring cup or small bowl and whisk in the arrowroot starch until well incorporated. Add to the onion mixture and cook, stirring frequently, until the almond milk has reduced and thickened, about 5 minutes. Stir in the chard and the optional nutmeg. Season with pepper to taste. Remove from the heat and serve at once.

Per serving: 124 calories, 3 g protein, 8 g fat (1 g sat), 11 g carbohydrates, 376 mg sodium, 281 mg calcium, 3 g fiber

Note: Analysis doesn't include nutmeg or freshly ground black pepper to taste.

green pea and edamame purée

WITH CARAMELIZED ONIONS

MAKES 4 SERVINGS

The flavors of green peas and edamame make an interesting combination, but this purée can also be made with green peas alone. The caramelized onions make a rich, striking counterpoint to the smooth purée, both in flavor and texture.

- 2 cups frozen **green peas**
- 2 cups frozen shelled **edamame** or additional frozen green peas
- 2 teaspoons chopped fresh **marjoram,** or ½ teaspoon dried
- ¾ cup unsweetened **almond milk** or Basic Almond Milk (page 9)
- ½ teaspoon **sea salt**
  Freshly ground **black pepper**
- ¼ cup **coconut oil,** plus more as needed
- 2 cups finely diced **onions**

Bring a large pot of water to a boil and add the peas and edamame. Return to a boil and cook until just tender, about 7 minutes. Drain well and transfer to a food processor. Add the marjoram and pulse until the peas and edamame are in small pieces. Scrape down the work bowl, add the almond milk and salt, and process until very smooth. If any bits of edamame skin remain, push the purée through a fine-mesh sieve to strain them out. Season with pepper to taste.

Put the oil in a medium saucepan over medium-high heat. When the oil is melted, add the onions and cook, stirring frequently, until soft and beginning to brown, about 10 minutes. If the onions are sticking, add 1 tablespoon of additional oil. Continue cooking, stirring constantly, until the onions are caramelized, about 10 minutes longer. Transfer the onions to a small bowl and cover to keep warm. Shortly before serving, put the purée in a medium saucepan and heat over medium heat, stirring constantly, until hot. To serve, form the purée into attractive mounds on individual plates. Make a small indentation in the top of the mounds with the back of a small spoon. Fill the indentations with the onions and a little of the cooking oil. Reserve the remaining oil for another use (it will be very flavorful). Serve at once.

Per serving: 345 calories, 164 g protein, 20 g fat (123 g sat), 28 g carbohydrates, 395 mg sodium, 185 mg calcium, 9 g fiber
Note: Analysis doesn't include freshly ground black pepper to taste.

mashed potatoes

MAKES 4 SERVINGS

Some foods are time-honored dishes in their own right as well as ideal accompaniments to other dishes. They can even make the perfect base for a sauce or gravy. Mashed potatoes are all that and more.

- 4 **medium Yukon gold or russet potatoes**
- 8 **tablespoons vegan butter**
- 1 **cup unsweetened almond milk or Rich Almond Milk** (page 10)
- ½ **teaspoon sea salt**
   Freshly ground black pepper

Peel the potatoes and cut them into 2-inch pieces. Put them in a medium saucepan and cover with water by about 1 inch. Bring to a boil over high heat. Decrease the heat to medium, cover, and cook until tender, about 30 minutes. To check if potatoes are done, insert a knife into the largest piece; the potato should slip off the knife easily.

Drain the potatoes and transfer to a medium bowl. Mash with a potato masher, fork, or silicone spatula until smooth. Add the butter, milk, and salt and stir to combine. Season with pepper to taste.

Per serving: 361 calories, 4 g protein, 23 g fat (6 g sat), 35 g carbohydrates, 533 mg sodium, 136 mg calcium, 5 g fiber

Note: Analysis doesn't include freshly ground black pepper to taste.

sweet potato purée

MAKES 4 SERVINGS

You can use regular orange sweet potatoes for this recipe or purple sweet potatoes, which are becoming more common on the produce shelf. Although both types are packed with nutrients and antioxidants, the deep purple ones add considerable visual interest to the plate.

1½ pounds orange or purple **sweet potatoes,** peeled and diced

½ teaspoon rubbed **sage**

¾ cup **Browned Garlic Cream** (page 16) or **Caramelized Onion Cream** (page 14)

¾ cup unsweetened **almond milk** or Basic Almond Milk (page 9)

¼ teaspoon **sea salt**

Freshly ground **black pepper**

2 teaspoons chopped fresh **parsley,** for garnish

Put the sweet potatoes in a large saucepan. Add water to cover by about 1 inch and bring to a boil over high heat. Decrease the heat to medium, cover, and cook until the sweet potatoes are very tender, about 30 minutes. Drain well. Transfer to a food processor, add the sage, and pulse 3 or 4 times. Scrape down the work bowl and add the garlic cream, almond milk, and salt. Process until very smooth. Season with pepper to taste. Transfer to the saucepan and heat over medium heat, stirring constantly, until hot. Garnish with the parsley and serve at once.

Per serving: 401 calories, 9 g protein, 29 g fat (9 g sat), 40 g carbohydrates, 371 mg sodium, 231 mg calcium, 6 g fiber

Note: Analysis doesn't include freshly ground black pepper to taste; analysis for the Browned Garlic Cream in this recipe is based on the almonds prior to straining.

ethiopian-style yams

MAKES 4 SERVINGS

The spices in this recipe lend an exciting twist. Baking the yams at a high temperature for a long period not only softens them but also deepens their flavor. The creamy sauce pulls everything together to make for one truly satisfying side dish.

3	pounds garnet yams or dark-orange **sweet potatoes**
2	tablespoons **coconut oil**
1¼	cups finely diced **onions**
4	cloves **garlic**, minced
1	teaspoon **paprika**
½	teaspoon **sea salt**
¼	teaspoon **cayenne**
¼	teaspoon ground **cinnamon**
¼	teaspoon ground **ginger**
¼	teaspoon ground **fenugreek** or **coriander**
1	cup unsweetened **almond milk** or Basic Almond Milk (page 9)
1	tablespoon freshly squeezed **lemon juice**

Preheat the oven to 400 degrees F. Line a rimmed baking sheet with foil.

Put the yams on the lined baking sheet and bake for 2 hours. Let cool completely, then peel and trim away any burned bits. Cut the flesh into bite-sized pieces.

Put the oil in a large saucepan over medium heat. When the oil is hot, add the onions and garlic and stir to combine. As soon as the onions begin to sizzle, decrease the heat to low, cover, and cook, stirring occasionally, for 10 minutes. If the onions are sticking, add 1 tablespoon of water. Add the paprika, salt, cayenne, cinnamon, ginger, and fenugreek and stir to combine. Increase the heat to medium and cook, stirring frequently, for 5 minutes. Stir in the almond milk and increase the heat to medium-high. Cook, stirring frequently, until thickened, about 10 minutes. Add the yams and lemon juice and cook, stirring occasionally and gently to coat with the sauce, until hot. Serve at once.

chef's note: Berbere is a peppery Ethiopian spice blend available at specialty food shops, and of course, Ethiopian markets. If you're able to find some, you can replace the paprika, salt, cayenne, cinnamon, ginger, and fenugreek with 2½ teaspoons of ground berbere. If you're not a big fan of spicy food, start with half of this amount, as you can always add more but you can't take it out.

The main fat in almonds is heart-healthy monounsaturated fat.

Per serving: 484 calories, 1 g protein, 8 g fat (6 g sat), 104 g carbohydrates, 350 mg sodium, 131 mg calcium, 13 g fiber

rutabaga mash

MAKES 4 SERVINGS

Rutabaga is a largely ignored vegetable, but unfairly so. Its flavor is unique and slightly sweet, with just a hint of bitterness in its skin. Properly cooked, rutabaga has a wonderfully smooth texture that's perfect for a mash.

2 pounds **rutabagas**

3 tablespoons extra-virgin **olive oil**

3 cloves **garlic**, minced

¼ teaspoon **sea salt**

1 cup **water**, plus more as needed

1 cup unsweetened **almond milk** or Rich Almond Milk (page 10)

2 tablespoons chopped fresh **parsley**

Freshly ground **black pepper**

Scrub the rutabagas and trim the tough ends. Peel if waxed. Cut into ½-inch cubes.

Put the oil, garlic, and salt in a medium saucepan over medium-low heat. Cook, stirring constantly, until the garlic begins to lightly brown, about 2 minutes. Add the rutabaga and cook, stirring constantly, until the cubes are evenly coated with the oil. Increase the heat to medium-high and add the water, stirring up any bits that may be stuck to the bottom of the pan. Cover and cook, stirring occasionally, until the rutabaga is tender, about 20 minutes. If the mixture becomes too dry, add ¼ cup of additional water.

When the rutabagas are done, decrease the heat to low and add the almond milk. Mash into a purée with a potato masher, fork, or silicone spatula. Stir in half the parsley and season with pepper to taste. Garnish with the remaining parsley and serve at once.

Per serving: 182 calories, 3 g protein, 11 g fat (2 g sat), 19 g carbohydrates, 227 mg sodium, 222 mg calcium, 6 g fiber
Note: Analysis doesn't include freshly ground black pepper to taste.

broccoli au gratin

Most gratins are made with cheese and a rich, creamy white sauce, but broccoli brings a bright aura of freshness and health to the mix.

- 6 tablespoons **vegan butter**
- 4 cups **broccoli florets**
- 3 tablespoons unbleached all-purpose **white flour**
- 1½ cups unsweetened **almond milk** or Rich Almond Milk (page 10)
- 8 ounces **vegan cheese**, grated
- ¼ teaspoon **sea salt**
- ¼ teaspoon freshly grated **nutmeg** or ground nutmeg
  Freshly ground **black pepper**

Preheat the oven to 400 degrees F. Grease a medium gratin dish or 6-cup baking dish with 1 tablespoon of the butter.

Steam the broccoli until tender-crisp, about 7 minutes. Refresh under cold running water and drain well.

Put 3 tablespoons of the butter in a small saucepan over medium-high heat. When the butter is melted, whisk in the flour. Cook, whisking almost constantly, until the mixture begins to brown lightly, 1½ to 2 minutes. Whisk in the almond milk and cook, whisking constantly, until the mixture thickens into a sauce, about 1 minute. Stir in about half the cheese and the salt and nutmeg. Gently stir in the broccoli. Season with pepper to taste.

Pour the broccoli mixture into the prepared gratin dish and smooth the top. Sprinkle the remaining cheese over the surface and dot with the remaining 2 tablespoons of butter. Bake for 20 minutes, until browned and bubbling. Serve at once.

CAULIFLOWER AU GRATIN: Replace the broccoli with 4 cups of cauliflower florets.

Per serving: 221 calories, 5 g protein, 16 g fat (4 g sat), 14 g carbohydrates, 413 mg sodium, 139 mg calcium, 4 g fiber
Note: Analysis doesn't include freshly ground black pepper to taste.

asparagus WITH SHIITAKE MUSHROOMS

MAKES 4 SERVINGS

This seasonal dish makes a succulent appetizer for an elegant, special-occasion meal.

 1 ounce dried **shiitake mushrooms**
 2 pounds **green asparagus**
 1½ tablespoons **coconut oil**
 ¼ cup finely diced **shallots** or onion
 ½ cup unsweetened **almond milk** or Basic Almond Milk (page 9)
 ¼ teaspoon **arrowroot starch**
 ¼ teaspoon **sea salt**
 3 tablespoons snipped fresh **chives**
 1 tablespoon freshly squeezed **lemon juice**
 Freshly ground **black pepper**

Put the mushrooms in a small bowl and cover with water. Let sit for at least 20 minutes to reconstitute. Transfer the mushrooms to a colander using a slotted spoon and reserve the soaking liquid. Rinse the mushrooms under cold running water to remove any embedded grit. Drain well. Pour the soaking liquid into a small bowl through a paper towel to filter out any grit.

Break off the woody ends of the asparagus. Trim the asparagus stalks if necessary so the asparagus are all fairly equal in length.

Put the oil in a medium skillet over medium heat. When the oil is melted, add the shallots. Cook, stirring frequently, until the shal-

lots are tender and translucent, about 5 minutes. Add the mushrooms and cook, stirring frequently, until the mushrooms have absorbed the oil and the shallots are beginning to brown, about 7 minutes. Add the mushroom soaking liquid and cook, stirring frequently, until the liquid is reduced to about 1 tablespoon, about 5 minutes. Put the almond milk in a measuring cup or small bowl and whisk in the arrowroot starch until well incorporated. Pour into the skillet and stir well. Stir in the salt. Decrease the heat to low and cover to keep warm.

Fill a large pot halfway with water and bring to a boil over high heat. Add the asparagus and cook until just tender but still firm, 4 to 7 minutes. Remove the asparagus with tongs and set them briefly on a clean tea towel to drain. Immediately divide the asparagus among four warmed plates, with the tips facing in the same direction.

Stir 2 tablespoons of the chives into the mushroom mixture. Add the lemon juice and stir again. Season with pepper to taste. Spoon the mushroom mixture across the center of the asparagus. Garnish with the remaining chives and serve at once.

Per serving: 164 calories, 7 g protein, 9 g fat (5 g sat), 17 g carbohydrates, 202 mg sodium, 117 mg calcium, 7 g fiber
Note: Analysis doesn't include freshly ground black pepper to taste.

cornbread

This recipe is flexible and forgiving. You can adapt it to your taste by adding one or more of the optional ingredients or keep it plain and straightforward without any extras at all. Your call.

- 6 tablespoons **vegan butter**
- ¾ cup unbleached all-purpose **white flour**
- 1 tablespoon **baking powder**
- 2 tablespoons unbleached **cane sugar**
- ¾ teaspoon **sea salt**
- 1¼ cups yellow **cornmeal**
- 1 cup sliced **scallions** (optional)
- 1 cup cooked fresh or frozen **corn** (optional)
- 1 cup grated **vegan cheese** (optional)
- ⅓ cup diced **jalapeño chiles** (optional)
- 1 cup unsweetened **almond milk** or Rich Almond Milk (page 10)
- 1½ teaspoons **Ener-G Egg Replacer** mixed with 2 tablespoons water until frothy

Preheat the oven to 425 degrees F. Grease a 9-inch square baking pan with 3 tablespoons of the butter. Put the dish in the oven to preheat.

Combine the flour, baking powder, sugar, and salt in a large bowl and whisk to combine. Add the cornmeal and whisk again. Add the optional ingredients of your choice and stir until evenly distributed.

Put the remaining 3 tablespoons of butter in a small saucepan over medium heat. When the butter is melted, remove from the heat and whisk in the milk and egg-replacer mixture. Pour into the dry ingredients and stir briefly, just until moistened. Immediately pour into the sizzling-hot baking pan and bake for 20 to 25 minutes, until puffed and lightly browned.

Per serving: 130 calories, 2 g protein, 6 g fat (1 g sat), 17 g carbohydrates, 309 mg sodium, 75 mg calcium, 1 g fiber

olive and herb crackers

MAKES 30 CRACKERS

This gluten-free cracker has a complex series of flavors that dance in and out of the foreground. If you can, substitute the dried herbes de Provence with three tablespoons of a mix of fresh parsley, sage, lavender, thyme, and rosemary for a real treat.

2 cups **almond pulp** (see page 63)

½ cup raw **pumpkin seeds**

24 **pitted olives**

½ cup **sesame seeds**

¼ cup **chickpea flour**

3 tablespoons extra-virgin **olive oil**

1 tablespoon **herbes de Provence**

1½ teaspoons **baking soda**

½ teaspoon **sea salt**

¼ teaspoon freshly ground **black pepper**

Preheat the oven to 325 degrees F. Lightly oil a sheet of parchment paper the size of a standard baking sheet.

Put all the ingredients in a food processor and pulse until blended and the pumpkin seeds are coarsely chopped. Transfer to the prepared parchment paper and pat into a rectangle. Roll out to the border of the parchment paper, about ⅛ inch thick. Cut into small rectangular crackers with a pizza cutter or sharp knife.

Lift the parchment paper with the crackers onto a baking sheet and bake for 15 minutes. Decrease the oven temperature to 200 degrees and bake for 3 hours, until the crackers are dry and crisp. Alternatively, put the crackers in a dehydrator set at 100 degrees and dehydrate for 8 to 12 hours.

Per cracker: 60 calories, 1 g protein, 6 g fat (1 g sat), 2 g carbohydrates, 149 mg sodium, 15 mg calcium, 1 g fiber

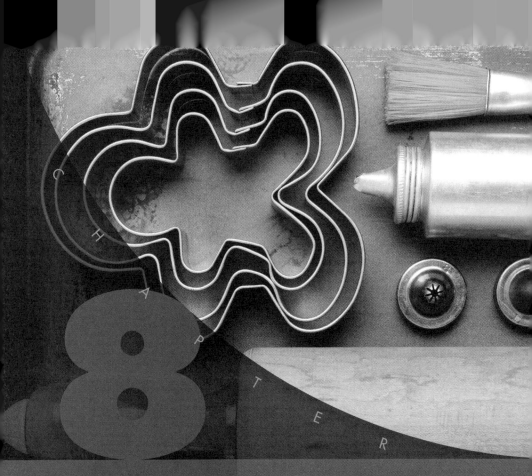

Sweet Tooth Central

kheer WITH ORANGE AND PISTACHIOS

MAKES 4 SERVINGS

Kheer is a traditional Indian rice pudding that can be served hot, warm, or chilled. This version includes orange zest, which is a newcomer on the scene.

    1 cup basmati rice
    1¾ cups water
       Pinch sea salt
    4 cups plain almond milk or Sweet Almond Milk
       (page 9), plus more as needed
    6 tablespoons unbleached cane sugar
    1 teaspoon vanilla extract
    1 teaspoon crushed cardamom seeds
       Grated zest of 1 orange
    ½ cup coarsely chopped unsalted roasted pistachios

Put the rice, water, and salt in a medium saucepan and bring to a boil over medium-high heat. Decrease the heat to low, cover, and cook for 20 minutes. Remove from the heat and let sit covered for 5 minutes. Fluff with a fork.

Add the almond milk, sugar, and vanilla extract to the rice and stir to combine. Bring to a boil over medium-high heat, stirring frequently. Decrease the heat to medium-low and cook, stirring occasionally, until almost all the liquid is absorbed, about 40 minutes. The mixture should be quite thick and creamy. Stir in the cardamom and cook, stirring constantly, for 1 minute longer. Remove from the heat and stir in the orange zest.

Serve hot or warm or transfer to a medium bowl and refrigerate until cold. If the kheer has thickened too much, stir in a little more almond milk to obtain the desired consistency. Just before serving, stir in half the pistachios. Garnish with the remaining pistachios.

Per serving: 346 calories, 7 g protein, 10 g fat (1 g sat), 55 g carbohydrates, 155 mg sodium, 470 mg calcium, 3 g fiber

cinnamon-cardamom rolls

Cardamom is an exotic east Asian spice, not well known or used in Western cuisines, but it did mysteriously find its way into traditional Swedish sweets. You can choose ground cardamom for ease, but nothing compares with the explosive flavor of freshly crushed cardamom seeds.

- 11 tablespoons soft **vegan butter**
- 3 cups unbleached all-purpose **white flour,** plus more as needed
- ¾ cup unbleached **cane sugar**
- 1 package (2.5 ounces) **or** 2¼ teaspoons **active dry yeast**
- 1 teaspoon **sea salt**
- ½ cup plus 2 tablespoons unsweetened **almond milk** or Rich Almond Milk (page 10)
- ½ cup **water**
- 1½ teaspoons ground **cinnamon**
- 1½ teaspoons crushed **cardamom seeds** or ground cardamom
- ¾ cup **powdered sugar**
- ½ teaspoon **vanilla extract**

Preheat the oven to 375 degrees F. Grease a 13 x 9-inch baking dish with 2 tablespoons of the butter.

Put 1 cup of the flour, ¼ cup of the sugar, and the yeast and salt in a medium bowl and stir to combine.

Put ½ cup of the almond milk and 4 tablespoons of the butter in a small saucepan over medium heat. When the butter is melted and the mixture reaches 120 to 130 degrees F, pour into the flour mixture and stir until moist. Add 1½ cups of the flour and stir until the mixture pulls away from the sides of the bowl, about 4 minutes. Add the remaining ½ cup of flour and knead until smooth, 8 to 10 minutes. If the mixture is too sticky, add up to ½ cup of additional flour. Cover and let rise in a warm spot until doubled in bulk, 45 to 60 minutes.

Punch the dough down and roll out on a lightly floured surface into a 20 x 12-inch rectangle. Spread with 4 tablespoons of the remaining butter. Put the remaining ½ cup of sugar and the cinnamon and cardamom in a small bowl and stir to combine. Sprinkle evenly over the buttered dough. Roll the dough up across the length to form a log. Cut the log into 1-inch-thick slices and put them cut-side down in the prepared baking dish, spacing them evenly about one-half inch apart. Cover with a clean tea towel and let rise for 45 minutes.

Bake for 25 to 30 minutes, until puffed and golden brown.

Put the powdered sugar, the remaining tablespoon of butter, the remaining 2 tablespoons of almond milk, and the vanilla extract in a small bowl. Stir until smooth. Drizzle over the rolls. Serve warm.

Per roll: 270 calories, 4 g protein, 11 g fat (3 g sat), 38 g carbohydrates, 288 mg sodium, 19 mg calcium, 1 g fiber

triple-chocolate muffins

At first glance, this recipe may look rather involved for a simple muffin, but rest assured, it's very easy. Even so, the results are impressive, especially the finishing touch of the chocolate glaze.

1½ cups **almond pulp** (see page 63)
⅓ cup **unsweetened cocoa powder**
1 cup plain **almond milk** or Rich Almond Milk (page 10)
¼ cup **sunflower oil**
2 teaspoons **vanilla extract**
1 teaspoon **almond extract**
1½ cups **unbleached all-purpose white flour**
¾ cup **light brown sugar**
1 tablespoon **baking powder**
1 teaspoon **baking soda**
1 teaspoon **sea salt**
1 cup **walnut pieces**
1 cup **semisweet chocolate chips**
4 ounces **dark chocolate,** chopped
6 tablespoons **vegan butter**
1 tablespoon **maple syrup**

Preheat the oven to 400 degrees F. Lightly oil a 12-cup standard muffin tin or line it with cupcake liners.

To make the muffins, put the almond pulp and cocoa powder in a medium bowl and knead them together with a silicone spatula or wooden spoon until well combined. Add the almond milk, oil, vanilla extract, and almond extract and stir until well combined.

Put the flour, sugar, baking powder, baking soda, and salt in a large bowl. Stir with a whisk to combine. Add the almond-pulp mixture and stir briefly, just until moistened. Fold in the walnuts and chocolate chips. Spoon equally into the prepared muffin cups and bake for 20 to 25 minutes, until a toothpick inserted in the center of a muffin comes out clean. Put the muffin tin on a cooling rack and let the muffins cool completely before removing them.

To make the glaze, put the chopped chocolate, butter, and maple syrup in a double boiler or small, heatproof bowl over a saucepan of warm (not hotter than 120 degrees F) water. Stir until the chocolate is melted and smooth. Invert a muffin and dip the top in the chocolate mixture, swirling gently to coat the top well. Repeat with the remaining muffins. Let rest until the glaze is set, about 10 minutes.

It's easy to measure a serving of almonds. There are 23 almonds in 1 ounce, and that's the perfect portion to munch on.

Per muffin: 468 calories, 7 g protein, 30 g fat (38 g sat), 45 g carbohydrates, 354 mg sodium, 118 mg calcium, 5 g fiber

mixed berry cobbler

MAKES 6 SERVINGS

This cobbler can be made with any combination of berries or even with just one variety if that's all you have available. In summer, when berries are plentiful, this is an ideal dessert to celebrate the season. In winter it can be made with frozen berries, and it will conjure up sunny afternoons with its warming richness.

- 6 cups **mixed berries**
- ¾ cup plus 3 tablespoons unbleached **cane sugar**
- 10 tablespoons **vegan butter,** cold
- 3 tablespoons **instant tapioca**
- 1 teaspoon grated **lemon zest**
- 2 tablespoons freshly squeezed **lemon juice**
- 1½ cups unbleached all-purpose **white flour,** plus more as needed
- 2 teaspoons **baking powder**
- 1 teaspoon **sea salt**
- ½ teaspoon **baking soda**
- ½ cup unsweetened **almond milk** or Rich Almond Milk (page 10)
- ¼ cup plain or vanilla coconut **yogurt** or soy yogurt

Preheat the oven to 375 degrees F.

To make the filling, put the berries, ½ cup of the sugar, 4 tablespoons of the butter, and the tapioca, lemon zest, and lemon juice in a large bowl and stir until well combined. Pour into a deep 8- or 10-cup baking dish and smooth the top. Bake for 20 to 25 minutes, until bubbling.

To make the topping, put the flour, ¼ cup of the sugar, and the baking powder, salt, and baking soda in a large bowl. Stir until well combined. Add the remaining 6 tablespoons of butter and cut it in using 2 knives, leaving pieces about the size of peas.

Put the almond milk and yogurt in a small bowl and whisk to combine. Add to the flour mixture and stir just until moistened. If the mixture is very sticky, add 1 to 2 tablespoons of additional flour.

Remove the berry mixture from the oven and immediately dot with the topping. Sprinkle with the remaining 3 tablespoons of sugar and return to the oven. Bake for 20 to 25 minutes, until the topping is golden and the cobbler is bubbling up through the gaps. Serve at once.

HOW TO REDUCE ALMOND MILK

Almond milk, even when thickeners and stabilizers have been added, behaves differently from its dairy counterpart. For example, almond milk can't be boiled down, or reduced, to thicken it the way that dairy milk or cream can. As it approaches about half the original volume, almond milk will break down rather than thicken further. Also, the color of almond milk tends to turn an unappetizing grayish color when boiled down. To counteract and prevent these effects to some degree, I recommend adding a small amount of arrowroot starch, which is a natural, easily digested thickener. This will produce the same effect that reduction produces in dairy milk, without the risk of ruining the dish.

Per serving: 463 calories, 3 g protein, 23 g fat (6 g sat), 58 g carbohydrates, 827 mg sodium, 128 mg calcium, 6 g fiber

pecan pie WITH PECAN CREAM

MAKES 8 SERVINGS

Pecan pie is a classic, and this version holds true to its roots. However, the pecan cream topping adds a unique alternative to standard whipped cream, transforming this pie into a regal standout.

1¼ cups unbleached all-purpose **white flour**

¾ teaspoon **sea salt**

7 tablespoons **vegan butter,** cold

3 tablespoons **ice water,** plus more as needed

¾ cup **maple syrup**

¾ cup plus 1 tablespoon **light brown sugar**

6 tablespoons **Ener-G Egg Replacer** mixed with ½ cup water until frothy

¼ cup **molasses**

1½ cups **raw pecans**

2 cups **roasted pecans**

2 cups plain **almond milk** or Rich Almond Milk (page 10)

⅛ teaspoon ground **cinnamon**

Preheat the oven to 400 degrees F.

To make the pie dough, put the flour and ½ teaspoon of the salt in a medium bowl. Cut the butter into tablespoon-sized pieces and add to the flour mixture. Pinch the butter into the flour and knead gently. A few teaspoon-sized pieces of butter should remain. Add the ice water and stir with a fork until the dough comes together. If the mixture is too dry, add a little more water, 1 teaspoon at a time, until a dough forms. Wrap the dough in plastic wrap and refrigerate for 30 to 60 minutes.

Gently knead the dough to form a flat disk. Roll out on a lightly floured surface to a thickness of about ⅛ inch. Gently transfer to a 9-inch pie pan. Curl the edges under and flute. Prick the bottom of the dough all over with a fork. Cover the dough with a sheet of foil and fill with ceramic pie weights or dried beans. Bake for 15 minutes. Remove the foil and weights and bake for 10 minutes longer. Remove from the oven and let cool completely on a rack.

To make the filling, put the maple syrup, ¾ cup of the sugar, the egg-replacer mixture, molasses, and remaining ¼ teaspoon of salt in a medium bowl and whisk until smooth and well combined. Stir in the raw pecans. Pour into the cooled pie shell and smooth the top. Bake for 25 minutes. Shake the pan gently. If the filling is loose, continue baking until set, up to 15 minutes longer. Remove from the oven and let cool on a rack.

To make the pecan cream, put the roasted pecans, almond milk, the remaining tablespoon of sugar, and the cinnamon in a blender and process on high speed until smooth. Press through a fine sieve to produce a smooth cream, or omit this step for a more rustic cream. Scrape into a pastry bag fitted with a medium star tip and pipe over the pie in a spiral pattern, beginning in the middle and radiating out to the edge. Alternatively, the cream can be spread over the top of the pie with an offset spatula or silicone spatula or spooned into a bowl and passed at the table.

Per serving: 686 calories, 6 g protein, 45 g fat (5 g sat), 73 g carbohydrates, 354 mg sodium, 400 mg calcium, 3 g fiber

pumpkin pie

Many people enjoy pumpkin pie as a dessert, but I think the ideal time for it is midafternoon, washed down with a stout cup of coffee. If you like, serve it with Almond Cream (page 11), plain or sweetened with a little maple syrup.

- 1¼ cups unbleached all-purpose **white flour**
- 1 teaspoon **sea salt**
- 7 tablespoons **vegan butter**, cold
- 3 tablespoons **ice water**, plus more as needed
- 2 cups canned **pumpkin purée**
- 1¼ cups plain **almond milk** or Rich Almond Milk (page 10)
- ½ cup unbleached **cane sugar**
- ⅓ cup **brown sugar**, packed
- 4½ teaspoons **Ener-G Egg Replacer** mixed with 6 tablespoons water until frothy
- 1 teaspoon ground **ginger**
- ½ teaspoon freshly grated **nutmeg** or ground nutmeg
- ¼ teaspoon ground **allspice**

Preheat the oven to 400 degrees F.

To make the pie dough, put the flour and ½ teaspoon of the salt in a medium bowl. Cut the butter into tablespoon-sized pieces and add to the flour mixture. Pinch the butter into the flour and knead gently. Some teaspoon-sized pieces of butter should remain. Add the ice water and stir with a fork until the dough comes together. If the mixture is too dry, add a little more water, 1 teaspoon at a time, until a dough forms. Wrap the dough in plastic wrap and refrigerate for 30 to 60 minutes.

While the pie dough is chilling, make the filling. Put the pumpkin, almond milk, sugar, brown sugar, egg-replacer mixture, ginger, nutmeg, remaining ½ teaspoon of salt, and the allspice in a medium bowl and whisk until well combined. Set aside.

Gently knead the dough to form a flat disk. Roll out on a lightly floured surface to a thickness of about ⅛ inch. Gently transfer to a 9-inch pie pan. Curl the edges under and flute. Prick the bottom of the dough all over with a fork. Cover the dough with a sheet of foil and fill with ceramic pie weights or dried beans. Bake for 15 minutes. Remove the foil and weights and bake for 10 minutes longer. Remove from the oven and immediately pour the pumpkin filling into the hot pie shell.

Decrease the oven temperature to 375 degrees F. Bake the pie for 35 to 45 minutes, until the filling is firm. Let cool completely on a rack before serving.

> **Almonds contain riboflavin and L-carnitine, nutrients that boost brain activity and may also reduce the risk of Alzheimer's disease.**

Per serving: 232 calories, 3 g protein, 10 g fat (3 g sat), 32 g carbohydrates, 398 mg sodium, 129 mg calcium, 1 g fiber

caramel sauce

MAKES 1½ CUPS

This dairy-free caramel sauce replicates the classic cream-based version in all respects. You won't believe how delicious it is!

1 cup unsweetened **almond milk,** Rich Almond Milk (page 10), **or Basic Almond Milk** (page 9)

½ teaspoon **arrowroot starch**

1½ cups **light brown sugar,** packed

½ cup **water**

1 tablespoon **coconut oil**

Put the almond milk and arrowroot starch in a small bowl or measuring cup and whisk until well combined.

Put the brown sugar and water in a small saucepan over medium-high heat. When the sugar has dissolved, begin stirring with a whisk. Monitor the mixture closely. It will already have a light brownish color, which will darken slightly as the sugar begins to caramelize. Observe the foam to see when it darkens more than the liquid. As soon as the mixture and foam reach a dark amber color (you may detect a caramel aroma), pour in the almond milk mixture, whisking very carefully and taking care to avoid the steam, which will be very hot. Continue whisking gently until all the solids have melted and a smooth sauce forms. Remove from the heat, add the oil, and whisk until well incorporated. Use the sauce at once or let cool, whisking occasionally. Stored in a tightly covered container in the refrigerator, the sauce will keep for 1 month.

Per 2 tablespoons: 81 calories, 0 g protein, 1 g fat (1 g sat), 17 g carbohydrates, 20 mg sodium, 40 mg calcium, 0 g fiber

espresso caramel sauce

MAKES 1¾ CUPS

The bitter edge of espresso does a fabulous job of cutting the sweetness of this sauce while simultaneously heightening the pleasure of the rich caramel.

- 1 cup unsweetened **almond milk,** Rich Almond Milk (page 10), **or Basic Almond Milk** (page 9)
- ½ teaspoon **arrowroot starch**
- 1½ cups **light brown sugar,** packed
- ½ cup **water**
- ⅓ cup **espresso coffee**
- 1 tablespoon **coconut oil**

Put the almond milk and arrowroot starch in a small bowl or measuring cup and whisk until well combined.

Put the brown sugar and water in a small saucepan over medium-high heat. When the sugar has dissolved, begin stirring with a whisk. Monitor the mixture closely. It will already have a light brownish color, which will darken slightly as the sugar begins to caramelize. Observe the foam to see when it darkens more than the liquid. As soon as the mixture and foam reach a dark amber color (you may detect a caramel aroma), pour in the almond milk mixture, whisking very carefully and taking care to avoid the steam, which will be very hot. Continue whisking gently until all the solids have melted and a smooth sauce forms. Remove from the heat, add the espresso and oil, and whisk until well incorporated. Use the sauce at once or let cool, whisking occasionally. Stored in a tightly covered container in the refrigerator, the sauce will keep for 1 month.

Per 2 tablespoons: 70 calories, 0 g protein, 1 g fat (1 g sat), 15 g carbohydrates, 18 mg sodium, 35 mg calcium, 0 g fiber

chocolate caramel sauce

MAKES 1⅔ CUPS

Combining chocolate and caramel is sublimely gratuitous. But then, that's what properly composed sweets are meant to be, right? This is marvelous warmed and drizzled over ice cream and then sprinkled with roasted nuts.

1 cup unsweetened **almond milk,** Rich Almond Milk (page 10), **or Basic Almond Milk** (page 9)

½ teaspoon **arrowroot starch**

1½ cups **light brown sugar,** packed

½ cup **water**

3 ounces **dark chocolate,** finely chopped

1 tablespoon **coconut oil**

Put the almond milk and arrowroot starch in a small bowl or measuring cup and whisk until well combined.

Put the brown sugar and water in a small saucepan over medium-high heat. When the sugar has dissolved, begin stirring with a whisk. Monitor the mixture closely. It will already have a light brownish color, which will darken slightly as the sugar begins to caramelize. Observe the foam to see when it darkens more than the liquid. As soon as the mixture and foam reach a dark amber color (you may detect a caramel aroma), pour in the almond milk mixture, whisking very carefully and taking care to avoid the steam, which will be very hot. Continue whisking gently until all the solids have melted and a smooth sauce forms. Remove from the heat, add the chocolate and oil, and whisk until well incorporated. Use the sauce at once or let cool, whisking occasionally. Stored in a tightly covered container in the refrigerator, the sauce will keep for 1 month.

Per 2 tablespoons: 108 calories, 0 g protein, 4 g fat (2 g sat), 20 g carbohydrates, 19 mg sodium, 36 mg calcium, 1 g fiber

mocha sauce

MAKES 1½ CUPS

Luxurious. Extravagant. Decadent. Guilty as charged. Glad to be of service.

- 1 cup unsweetened **almond milk,** Rich Almond Milk
  (page 10), **or Basic Almond Milk** (page 9)
- ½ teaspoon **arrowroot starch**
- ¼ cup unbleached **cane sugar**
- ¼ cup **espresso coffee**
- 4 ounces **dark chocolate,** finely chopped
- 1 tablespoon **coconut oil**

Put the almond milk and arrowroot starch in a small saucepan and whisk until well combined. Bring to a simmer over medium-high heat, whisking constantly, until thickened, about 5 minutes. Add the sugar and espresso and whisk until thoroughly blended. Remove from the heat and whisk in the chocolate and oil. Use at once or pour into a clean glass jar and let cool. Covered tightly and stored in the refrigerator, the sauce will keep for 2 weeks. Reheat to a pourable consistency before serving.

Almonds have the distinct honor of being one of the few proteins and the only nut that is alkaline forming.

Per 2 tablespoons: 65 calories, 1 g protein, 4 g fat (3 g sat), 6 g carbohydrates, 14 mg sodium, 25 mg calcium, 1 g fiber

hot fudge sauce

MAKES 1½ CUPS

If you're looking for a classic killer chocolate sauce, this is it. I used to make it with cream and butter; now I make it with almond milk and coconut oil. It tastes exactly the same. How many things do you know of that are that reliable?

1 cup unsweetened **almond milk,** Rich Almond Milk (page 10), **or Basic Almond Milk** (page 9)

1 cup unbleached **cane sugar**

¾ cup unsweetened Dutch-processed **cocoa powder**

1 teaspoon **instant coffee** granules or powder (optional)

¼ cup **coconut oil**

Put the almond milk, sugar, cocoa, and optional instant coffee in a small saucepan and whisk to combine. Cook over medium-high heat, whisking constantly, until the sugar, cocoa, and coffee have dissolved. Add the oil and whisk until smooth. Use at once or transfer to a clean jar and let cool. Covered tightly and stored in the refrigerator, the sauce will keep for 1 month. Reheat to a pourable consistency before serving.

ALLERGEN ALERT

If you are allergic to any type of tree nut, you should also avoid almonds and almond products, including almond milk. A person who is allergic to one type of tree nut has a higher chance of being allergic to other types. Tree nuts include, but aren't limited to, almonds, Brazil nuts, cashew nuts, hazelnuts, pistachio nuts, and walnuts.

Per 2 tablespoons: 70 calories, 1 g protein, 5 g fat (4 g sat), 7 g carbohydrates, 14 mg sodium, 31 mg calcium, 1 g fiber

chocolate ganache

MAKES 1½ CUPS

Ganache is the traditional filling for chocolate truffles and tarts. When it has cooled but not solidified, it can be whipped to make a light and airy frosting for cakes. It can also be stirred into soft ice cream to make a chocolate swirl. Oh, and just so you know, it can be eaten with a spoon too.

- 8 ounces **dark chocolate,** coarsely chopped
- 1 cup unsweetened **almond milk,** Rich Almond Milk (page 10), **or Basic Almond Milk** (page 9)

Put the chocolate in a medium bowl. Put the almond milk in a small saucepan and bring to a simmer over medium-high heat. Remove from the heat and wait until the milk stops bubbling, about 15 seconds. Pour over the chocolate and whisk until smooth. Use at once or transfer to a clean glass jar and let cool. Covered tightly and stored in the refrigerator, the ganache will keep for 2 weeks.

Per 2 tablespoons: 105 calories, 1 g protein, 6 g fat (3 g sat), 11 g carbohydrates, 14 mg sodium, 23 mg calcium, 1 g fiber

pistachio cream

MAKES 1½ CUPS

Mildly sweet, this cream embodies the spirit of pistachios in cloud form. It makes a unique, light sauce for chocolate desserts, and its flavor blends well with certain fruits, such as apricots, figs, peaches, and pears.

- 1 cup shelled **unsalted roasted pistachios**
- ½ cup unsweetened **almond milk,** Rich Almond Milk (page 10), **or Basic Almond Milk** (page 9)
- 2 tablespoons **powdered sugar**
- ⅛ teaspoon **pistachio extract** (optional)

Put the pistachios in a heatproof bowl and cover with boiling water. Let sit for 2 hours, then drain. Slip off the skins and discard.

Put the pistachios, almond milk, powdered sugar, and optional pistachio extract in a blender and process on high speed until smooth. Use at once or transfer to a clean glass jar. Covered tightly and stored in the refrigerator, the cream will keep for 1 week.

The phosphorus in almonds helps build strong bones and teeth.

Per 2 tablespoons: 65 calories, 2 g protein, 4 g fat (0.4 g sat), 4 g carbohydrates, 13 mg sodium, 35 mg calcium, 1 g fiber

chocolate-amaretto truffles

MAKES 30 TRUFFLES

Melt-in-your-mouth almond-flavored truffles. Pace yourself. Or not. Really, no one is going to monitor your chocolate habits, so do whatever seems right to you. I'm just the enabler.

- 8 ounces **dark chocolate,** coarsely chopped
- 1 cup plain **almond milk** or Sweet Almond Milk (page 9)
- ½ teaspoon **almond extract**
- ½ cup unsweetened Dutch-processed **cocoa powder**

Put the chocolate in a medium bowl. Put the almond milk in a small saucepan and bring to a simmer over medium-high heat. Remove from the heat and wait until the milk stops bubbling, about 15 seconds. Pour over the chocolate and whisk until smooth. Whisk in the almond extract. Let cool completely.

Line a baking sheet with waxed paper or parchment paper. Put the cocoa in a wide, shallow bowl. Scoop out about 1½ tablespoons of the chocolate mixture and form it into a ball with your hands. Drop the ball into the cocoa and roll it around to coat it evenly. Set the ball on the lined baking sheet. Repeat with the remaining chocolate mixture. Cover the truffles with plastic wrap and put them in the refrigerator to firm up, about 1 hour. Once the truffles are firm, remove them from the refrigerator and let them come to room temperature before serving.

TIP You will have some cocoa left over. Sift it through a fine sieve to remove any bits of chocolate and store it for another use.

Per truffle: 46 calories, 1 g protein, 3 g fat (2 g sat), 6 g carbohydrates, 5 mg sodium, 17 mg calcium, 1 g fiber

chocolate-ginger truffles

MAKES 30 TRUFFLES

When you slip one of these truffles into your mouth, let it slowly melt on your tongue rather than bite into it. This will greatly enhance your truffle experience.

8 ounces **dark chocolate,** coarsely chopped

1 cup plain **almond milk** or Sweet Almond Milk (page 9)

1 tablespoon peeled and finely grated fresh **ginger**

½ teaspoon **rum extract**

½ cup unsweetened Dutch-processed **cocoa powder**

Put the chocolate in a medium bowl. Put the almond milk in a small saucepan and bring to a simmer over medium-high heat. Remove from the heat and wait until the milk stops bubbling, about 15 seconds. Pour over the chocolate and whisk until smooth. Add the ginger and rum extract and whisk again. Let cool completely.

Line a baking sheet with waxed paper or parchment paper. Put the cocoa in a wide, shallow bowl. Scoop out about 1½ tablespoons of the chocolate mixture and form it into a ball with your hands. Drop the ball into the cocoa and roll it around to coat it evenly. Set the ball on the lined baking sheet. Repeat with the remaining chocolate mixture. Cover the truffles with plastic wrap and put them in the refrigerator to firm up, about 1 hour. Once the truffles are firm, remove them from the refrigerator and let them come to room temperature before serving.

Per truffle: 45 calories, 1 g protein, 3 g fat (2 g sat), 5 g carbohydrates, 5 mg sodium, 16 mg calcium, 1 g fiber

chocolate-orange truffles

MAKES 30 TRUFFLES

This is the classic flavor, the original *truffe au chocolat*, created to mimic the look of a real truffle, freshly dug in the fall from under an oak tree in the Périgord. The French love to make food look like something else, just to mess with your mind a little and show off their incomparable skills.

- 8 ounces **dark chocolate,** coarsely chopped
- 1 cup plain **almond milk** or Sweet Almond Milk (page 9)
- 1 teaspoon very finely grated **orange zest**
- ½ teaspoon **orange extract**
- ½ cup unsweetened Dutch-processed **cocoa powder**

Put the chocolate in a medium bowl. Put the almond milk in a small saucepan and bring to a simmer over medium-high heat. Remove from the heat and wait until the milk stops bubbling, about 15 seconds. Pour over the chocolate and whisk until smooth. Add the orange zest and orange extract and whisk again. Let cool completely.

Line a baking sheet with waxed paper or parchment paper. Put the cocoa in a wide, shallow bowl. Scoop out about 1½ tablespoons of the chocolate mixture and form it into a ball with your hands. Drop the ball into the cocoa and roll it around to coat it evenly. Set the ball on the lined baking sheet. Repeat with the remaining chocolate mixture. Cover the truffles with plastic wrap and put them in the refrigerator to firm up, about 1 hour. Once the truffles are firm, remove them from the refrigerator and let them come to room temperature before serving.

SPICY CHOCOLATE-ORANGE TRUFFLES: Add ¼ to ½ teaspoon of cayenne along with the orange zest and orange extract.

Per truffle: 46 calories, 1 g protein, 3 g fat (2 g sat), 6 g carbohydrates, 5 mg sodium, 17 mg calcium, 1 g fiber

chocolate-mint truffles

MAKES 30 TRUFFLES

People have asked me which flavor of truffle is my favorite, and my answer is always straight to the point: chocolate. The core flavor of truffles is always chocolate, but variations spice it up a bit. These are mint. Read on to discover my secret for how best to infuse this flavor into the chocolate.

> 8 ounces **dark chocolate,** coarsely chopped
> 1 cup plain **almond milk** or Sweet Almond Milk (page 9)
> ½ cup fresh **mint leaves,** firmly packed
> ½ teaspoon **peppermint extract**
> ½ cup unsweetened Dutch-processed **cocoa powder**

Put the chocolate in a medium bowl. Put the almond milk in a small saucepan and bring to a simmer over medium-high heat. Remove from the heat, add the mint leaves, and stir until well combined. Let sit for 4 minutes. Strain through a fine-mesh sieve, pressing down firmly on the leaves to extract as much liquid as possible. Measure the milk again and add more if necessary to make 1 cup. Return to the saucepan and reheat over medium heat. Do not boil. When the milk is hot to the touch, pour over the chocolate and whisk until smooth. Add the peppermint extract and whisk again. Let cool completely.

Line a baking sheet with waxed paper or parchment paper. Put the cocoa in a wide, shallow bowl. Scoop out about 1½ tablespoons of the chocolate mixture and form it into a ball with your hands. Drop the ball into the cocoa and roll it around to coat it evenly. Set the ball on the lined baking sheet. Repeat with the remaining chocolate mixture. Cover the truffles with plastic wrap and put them in the refrigerator to firm up, about 1 hour. Once the truffles are firm, remove them from the refrigerator and let them come to room temperature before serving.

Per truffle: 46 calories, 1 g protein, 3 g fat (2 g sat), 6 g carbohydrates, 5 mg sodium, 17 mg calcium, 1 g fiber

chocolate-almond ice cream

MAKES 1 QUART

I'm a shameless chocoholic, it's true, and this is admittedly among the best chocolate dishes I've ever made. If you seriously like chocolate, this one's for you.

- 1 cup natural or blanched **almonds**
- 2¼ cups unsweetened **almond milk,** Rich Almond Milk (page 10), **or Basic Almond Milk** (page 9)
- ¾ cup **maple syrup**
- ¾ cup unsweetened Dutch-processed **cocoa powder**
- 4 ounces very **dark chocolate,** chopped
- 1 tablespoon **coconut oil**
- 1 teaspoon **almond extract**
- 1 teaspoon **vanilla extract**

Preheat the oven to 400 degrees F. Spread the almonds in a single layer on a baking sheet and bake for 10 minutes. Transfer to a plate to cool. Chop the almonds very coarsely, just in half or thirds.

Put the almond milk and maple syrup in a medium saucepan. Bring to a simmer over medium-high heat. Immediately add the cocoa and whisk until dissolved. Remove from the heat and add the chocolate, oil, almond extract, and vanilla extract. Whisk until smooth. Pour into a medium bowl and let cool. Cover with plastic wrap and refrigerate until cold, about 2 hours.

Pour the mixture into an ice-cream machine and freeze according to the manufacturer's instructions. When the ice cream is thick but still soft, stir in the almonds. Scrape into a container and freeze until firm.

Per ½ cup: 273 calories, 5 g protein, 14 g fat (5 g sat), 36 g carbohydrates, 49 mg sodium, 145 mg calcium, 5 g fiber

caramel-pecan ice cream

MAKES 1 QUART

You've never had an ice cream quite as amazing as this. No, really, you haven't. Before I created this recipe, I hadn't either.

- 2 cups raw **pecans**
- 2½ cups unsweetened **almond milk,** Rich Almond Milk (page 10), **or** Basic Almond Milk (page 9)
- ¾ cup plus 2 tablespoons **Caramel Sauce** (page 126), **at** room temperature
- ¾ cup **maple syrup**
- 2 tablespoons **coconut oil**
- 1 tablespoon **vanilla extract**

Preheat the oven to 400 degrees F. Spread the pecans in a single layer on a baking sheet and bake for 7 minutes. Transfer to a plate to cool. Lightly crush 1 cup of the pecans and set aside. Put the remaining pecans in a blender.

Add the almond milk, ½ cup of the caramel sauce, and the maple syrup, oil, and vanilla extract to the pecans in the blender and process on high speed until smooth. Pour into a medium bowl, cover with plastic wrap, and refrigerate until cold, about 2 hours.

Pour the pecan mixture into an ice-cream machine and freeze according to the manufacturer's instructions. When the ice cream is thick but still soft, stir in the crushed pecans. Make an indentation in the surface of the ice cream and pour in the remaining caramel sauce. Swirl the caramel sauce into the ice cream using a table knife or narrow spatula, taking care not to overmix it. Scrape the ice cream into a container and freeze until firm.

Per ½ cup: 366 calories, 3 g protein, 25 g fat (3 g sat), 39 g carbohydrates, 67 mg sodium, 144 mg calcium, 0 g fiber

chocolate-caramel ice cream WITH WALNUTS

MAKES 1 QUART

Without the walnuts, this ice cream might almost be unbearably rich and sweet, but the nuts contribute a hint of astringency and bitterness that perfectly balances the sweetness.

2½   cups unsweetened **almond milk,** Rich Almond Milk (page 10), **or** Sweet Almond Milk (page 9)

1¼   teaspoons **arrowroot starch**

1¼   cups **Chocolate Caramel Sauce** (page 128), **at room temperature**

2   tablespoons **coconut oil**

½   cup **walnut pieces**

Put the almond milk and arrowroot starch in a medium saucepan and whisk to combine. Cook over medium-high heat, whisking constantly, until thickened, about 3 minutes. Remove from the heat, add the Chocolate Caramel Sauce, and whisk until smooth. Pour into a medium bowl and whisk in the oil. Cover with plastic wrap and refrigerate until cold, about 2 hours.

Pour the mixture into an ice-cream machine and freeze according to the manufacturer's instructions. When the ice cream is thick but still soft, stir in the walnuts. Serve at once or scrape into a container and freeze until firm.

Per ½ cup: 233 calories, 2 g protein, 9 g fat (5 g sat), 26 g carbohydrates, 71 mg sodium, 144 mg calcium, 2 g fiber

raspberry-lemon ice cream

MAKES 1 QUART

To keep my desserts from being too cloying, I try to balance them with a little bitterness or tartness. Raspberries usually bring a touch of tartness with them, but just to make sure, I add a splash of fresh lemon juice. For this ice cream, I also included the zest, allowing the lemon to share center stage.

- 1 **pound frozen raspberries**
- 2 **cups unsweetened almond milk,** Rich Almond Milk (page 10), **or Basic Almond Milk** (page 9)
- ½ **cup unbleached cane sugar**
- 2 **tablespoons coconut oil**
- 2 **teaspoons grated lemon zest** (remove the zest before juicing the lemon)
- 1 **tablespoon freshly squeezed lemon juice**

Put all the ingredients in a blender and process on high speed until smooth. Pour into a medium bowl, cover with plastic wrap, and refrigerate until cold, about 2 hours.

Pour the mixture into an ice-cream machine and freeze according to the manufacturer's instructions. Serve at once or scrape into a container and freeze until firm.

Per ½ cup: 113 calories, 1 g protein, 5 g fat (3 g sat), 19 g carbohydrates, 41 mg sodium, 89 mg calcium, 4 g fiber

mocha chip ice cream

MAKES 1 QUART

I think there's no better culinary pairing than the fruit of these two dark-roasted beans: chocolate and coffee. If you agree, this ice cream is guaranteed to make you swoon.

> 3 cups unsweetened **almond milk,** Rich Almond Milk (page 10), **or Basic Almond Milk** (page 9)
>
> 1½ teaspoons **arrowroot starch**
>
> ½ cup unbleached **cane sugar**
>
> ½ cup **espresso coffee**
>
> 8 ounces **dark chocolate,** finely chopped
>
> 3 tablespoons **coconut oil**
>
> ½ cup coarsely chopped **dark chocolate** or raw cacao nibs

Put the almond milk and arrowroot in a small saucepan and whisk until well combined. Bring to a simmer over medium-high heat, whisking constantly. When the milk thickens, add the sugar and espresso, whisking until thoroughly blended. Remove from the heat, add the finely chopped chocolate, and whisk until smooth. Whisk in the oil. Pour into a medium bowl, cover with plastic wrap, and refrigerate until cold, about 2 hours.

Pour the mixture into an ice-cream machine and freeze according to the manufacturer's instructions. When the ice cream is thick but still soft, stir in the coarsely chopped chocolate. Serve at once or scrape into a container and freeze until firm.

Per ½ cup: 335 calories, 3 g protein, 20 g fat (13 g sat), 38 g carbohydrates, 62 mg sodium, 133 mg calcium, 4 g fiber

baked-apple ice cream

MAKES 1 QUART

This sweet treat combines two dessert favorites: vanilla ice cream and baked apples with walnuts. It's a seasonal delight, which means it's perfect to serve any season of the year. Try it as a holiday treat or any time apples and cinnamon beckon.

- ⅔ cup unbleached **cane sugar**
- 2 tablespoons **coconut oil**
  Finely grated zest of 1 **lemon** (remove the zest before juicing the lemon)
- ½ teaspoon ground **cinnamon**
- ⅓ cup coarsely chopped **walnuts**
- 2 tablespoons **dried currants**
- 4 small **apples,** cored
  Juice of 1 **lemon**
- ¼ cup **water**
- 1 cup unsweetened **almond milk** or Basic Almond Milk (page 9)
- ½ cup **Almond Cream** (page 11)
- 1 teaspoon **vanilla extract**

Preheat the oven to 375 degrees F.

Put 2 tablespoons of the sugar and the oil, lemon zest, and cinnamon in a medium bowl and stir until well combined. Mix in the walnuts and currants until evenly distributed. Stuff the mixture into the cavities of the apples, piling any excess on the tops. Put the apples in an 8-inch baking dish. Sprinkle the lemon juice evenly over the apples and pour the water around them. Cover the dish and bake for 1 hour.

When the apples are cool enough to handle, remove the skins and any flesh clinging to them and put them in a blender. Tip the baking dish and pour the accumulated juices into the blender, reserving the apple flesh, walnuts, and currants. Add the almond milk, almond cream, the remaining sugar, and the vanilla extract to the blender and process on high speed until smooth. Pour the mixture into a medium bowl. Mash the baked apple flesh coarsely and add it to the bowl along with the walnuts and currants. Mix well. Cover with plastic wrap and refrigerate until cold, about 2 hours.

Pour the mixture into an ice-cream machine and freeze according to the manufacturer's instructions. Serve at once or scrape into a container and freeze until firm.

Almonds have more protein and fiber than any other tree nut, which makes them particularly filling and satisfying.

Per ½ cup: 223 calories, 3 g protein, 13 g fat (3 g sat), 6 g carbohydrates, 21 mg sodium, 86 mg calcium, 3 g fiber

Note: Analysis for the Almond Cream in this recipe is based on the almonds prior to straining.

bing cherry ice cream

MAKES 1 QUART

Almond milk makes a spectacular alliance with sweet, ripe cherries in this luscious frozen dessert.

3 cups fresh or thawed frozen pitted **Bing cherries**

2 cups unsweetened **almond milk,** Rich Almond Milk (page 10), **or** Basic Almond Milk (page 9)

⅔ cup maple syrup or unbleached **cane sugar**

¼ cup **coconut oil**

1 teaspoon **vanilla extract**

Put 2 cups of the cherries and the almond milk, maple syrup, oil, and vanilla extract in a blender and process on high speed until smooth. Pour into a medium bowl, cover with plastic wrap, and refrigerate until cold, about 2 hours.

Pour the mixture into an ice-cream machine and freeze according to the manufacturer's instructions.

Coarsely chop the remaining cup of cherries and fold them into the mixture. Serve at once or scrape into a container and freeze until firm. For the best results, move from the freezer to the refrigerator about 15 minutes before serving to soften slightly.

CHOCOLATE-CHERRY ICE CREAM: Fold in ½ cup of coarsely chopped dark chocolate along with the chopped cherries.

Per ½ cup: 170 calories, 1 g protein, 8 g fat (6 g sat), 27 g carbohydrates, 42 mg sodium, 100 mg calcium, 14 g fiber

nectarine sherbet

MAKES 4 SERVINGS

When nectarines are ripe and at their peak of flavor, the best way to enjoy them is simply to eat them straight up. But when they're plentiful, you can capture their perfection in this light, refreshing sherbet.

    3   large yellow or white **nectarines,** diced (see chef's note)
    1½ cups plain **almond milk** or Sweet Almond Milk
        (page 9)
    ⅓   cup unbleached **cane sugar**
    1   tablespoon freshly squeezed **lemon juice**
    ½   vanilla bean, or ½ teaspoon **vanilla extract**

Put the nectarines, almond milk, sugar, and lemon juice in a blender. Cut the vanilla bean in half lengthwise. Scrape out the seeds and add to the blender. Process on high speed until smooth. Pour into a medium bowl, cover with plastic wrap, and refrigerate until cold, about 2 hours.

Pour the mixture into an ice-cream machine and freeze according to the manufacturer's instructions. Serve at once or scrape into a container and freeze until firm. For the best results, move from the freezer to the refrigerator about 15 minutes before serving to soften slightly.

TIP Stored in the freezer, this sherbet will retain its delectable quality for at least 1 month.

chef's note: White nectarines, like white peaches, have a heavenly aroma when perfectly ripe and a rich, full-bodied flavor. It's best to peel white nectarines before using in recipes because the skin will give dishes an unappealing brownish color. Yellow nectarines need not be peeled, as their yellow flesh combines well with the color of their skin.

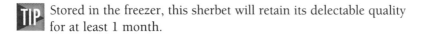

Per serving: 140 calories, 2 g protein, 1 g fat (0 g sat), 18 g carbohydrates, 56 mg sodium, 175 mg calcium, 2 g fiber

caramelized figs WITH ALMOND CREAM

This very simple dessert needs only a little foresight, yet the happy memories of it will remain with your guests for a good long while.

- 1 **cup blanched almonds, soaked in water 8 to 12 hours and drained**
- 1 **cup plain almond milk or Sweet Almond Milk** (page 9)
- 5 **tablespoons unbleached cane sugar**
- ¼ **teaspoon almond extract**
- 1 **tablespoon coconut oil**
- 16 **ripe fresh figs, stemmed and cut in half lengthwise**
- 4 **sprigs fresh mint** (optional)

Put the almonds, almond milk, 3 tablespoons of the sugar, and the almond extract in a blender and process on high speed until smooth. Divide the mixture among four plates, spreading it out into shallow pools in the center of each plate.

Put the remaining 2 tablespoons of sugar on a small plate. Put the oil in a large skillet and melt it over high heat. Dip the cut sides of the figs in the sugar, then set them in the skillet cut-side down and cook for 1 minute. Stir gently to toss the figs and cook for 1 minute longer. Divide the figs among the plates, forming attractive piles in the center of the almond cream. Garnish with the optional mint sprigs and serve at once.

Per serving: 432 calories, 8 g protein, 22 g fat (4 g sat), 56 g carbohydrates, 48 mg sodium, 191 mg calcium, 4 g fiber

caramelized bananas

WITH ALMOND CREAM AND CHOCOLATE DRIZZLE

MAKES 4 SERVINGS

Bananas are an undervalued commodity when it comes to dessert, but when the dessert is properly planned and executed, bananas can indeed be stars. Of course, it always helps to have a little chocolate included.

- ¼ cup unbleached cane sugar
- 4 teaspoons crushed cardamom seeds
- 1 tablespoon coconut oil, plus more as needed
- 4 bananas, cut in half lengthwise
- ¾ cup Almond Cream (page 11) or Pistachio Cream (page 132)
- ¼ cup Hot Fudge Sauce (page 130), warmed
- ¼ cup coarsely chopped unsalted roasted pistachios

Put the sugar and cardamom in a small bowl and stir to combine. Pour onto a large plate and spread out evenly.

Put 1 tablespoon of the oil in a large skillet and melt over medium-high heat. Put a banana half cut-side down in the sugar and press gently to coat the cut side. Put the banana half in the skillet, cut-side down. Repeat with as many banana halves as will fit comfortably in the skillet and cook for 1½ minutes. Turn the bananas over and cook the other side for 1 minute. Carefully remove the bananas from the skillet and put them on a plate. Cover them to keep warm and repeat with the remaining bananas, adding more coconut oil to the skillet if needed. When all the bananas have been caramelized, divide them among four plates, arranging them artfully.

Put a dollop of the almond cream next to the bananas and drizzle about 1 tablespoon of the warm fudge sauce back and forth across them. Sprinkle each serving with 1 tablespoon of the pistachios and serve at once.

Per serving: 453 calories, 9 g protein, 29 g fat (8 g sat), 47 g carbohydrates, 11 mg sodium, 146 mg calcium, 8 g fiber

Note: Analysis for the Almond Cream in this recipe is based on the almonds prior to straining.

roasted pears WITH ALMOND CREAM AND PINE NUTS

MAKES 4 SERVINGS

In late fall when pears are in season, this a stupendous dessert to offer guests. Try it at a holiday meal in place of all those heavy pies.

- 4 ripe Bartlett or Anjou **pears**
- 4 teaspoons unbleached **cane sugar**
- ½ teaspoon ground **allspice**
- ½ teaspoon ground **ginger**
- 2 tablespoons **coconut oil**
- 1½ cups **Almond Cream** (page 11)
- ¼ cup **Caramel Sauce** (page 126) or **Chocolate Caramel Sauce** (page 128), **warmed**
- ¼ cup fresh or thawed frozen **blackberries,** juice reserved

Preheat the oven to 450 degrees F.

Peel the pears and cut in half lengthwise. Scoop out the seeds using a melon baller, making an attractive round hole. (You can use a spoon instead of a melon baller, but the hole won't be as attractively round.) Turn the pear halves cut-side down and cut them in half lengthwise again. Cut away the stem section with a paring knife.

Combine the sugar, allspice, and ginger in a large bowl and mix well. Add the pears and toss very gently with the sugar mixture until lightly coated.

Put the oil in a large, ovenproof skillet over medium-high heat. When the oil is melted, add the pears, cut-side down. Cook the pears for 3 minutes. Turn the pears and cook the other cut side until brown, about 3 minutes. Turn the pears so the two browned sides are facing up. Put the skillet in the oven and bake for 7 minutes.

Put one-quarter of the almond cream in the center of each of four large plates. Arrange four of the pear quarters on the plate, radiating them out from the center like the points of a compass, with the bottoms just touching the cream. Drizzle the caramel sauce between the pears in a decorative pattern. If using thawed frozen blackberries, toss them briefly with their juice. Garnish the plates with the fresh berries or the thawed berries and their juice.

TIP If you don't have an oven-proof skillet large enough for all the pears, put a large baking dish in the oven when you begin the initial browning process of the pears, and then transfer the pears to the dish and proceed with the recipe.

Per serving: 482 calories, 13 g protein, 34 g fat (8 g sat), 37 g carbohydrates, 2 mg sodium, 243 mg calcium, 12 g fiber
Note: Analysis for the Almond Cream in this recipe is based on the almonds prior to straining.

Suppliers

ALMONDS

essentiallivingfoods.com
homegrownalmonds.com
livingnutz.com
nuts.com
organicalmondsraw.com
sunfood.com
terrasoul.com
znaturalfoods.com

HIGH-SPEED BLENDERS

blendtec.com
vitamix.com

NUT MILK BAGS

amazon.com
ecopeaceful.com/products
purejoyplanet.com
rawnutmilkbag.com

ABOUT THE AUTHOR

Alan Roettinger is a writer, food designer, blogger, and public speaker. He has been a private chef to the stars for over thirty years, serving a broad spectrum of high-profile clients, from entertainers to presidents.

Throughout his years as a private chef, Alan developed a reputation for working within the limitations of restricted diets to create delicious food tailored to specific tastes. His primary focus is bringing health and pleasure together in food.

Alan's first cookbook, *Omega-3 Cuisine,* offers a wide range of dishes that are simultaneously exotic and accessible to the home cook. His second cookbook, *Speed Vegan*, offers quick, easy, plant-based dishes with unusual flavors for the time-pressured home cook. In his third book, *Extraordinary Vegan,* he continues the theme of combining health with pleasure, taking this combo beyond the ordinary to new heights. And in his fourth book, *Paleo Vegan,* coauthored with Ellen Jaffe Jones, Alan brings together two popular, diverse eating styles and showcases their surprising compatibilities.

Visit him at alanroettinger.com.

Index

Recipe titles appear in *italics*.

BookPublishing Co.

books that educate, inspire, and empower

To find your favorite books on plant-based cooking and nutrition,
living foods lifestyle, and healthy living, visit:
BookPubCo.com

Extraordinary Vegan
Alan Roettinger
978-1-57067-296-5 • $19.95

Paleo Smoothies
Alan Roettinger
978-1-57067-316-0 • $5.95

Paleo Vegan
Ellen Jaffe Jones,
Recipes by Alan Roettinge
978-1-57067-305-4 • $16.95

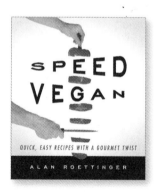

Speed Vegan
Allen Roettinger
978-1-57067-244-6 • $19.95

Artisan Vegan Cheese
Miyoko Schinner
978-1-57067-283-5 • $19.95

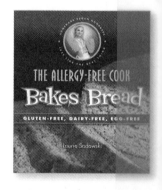

The Allergy-Free Cook
Bakes Bread
Laurie Sadowski
978-1-57067-262-0 • $14.95